IMAGES OF WAR

CHIANG KAI-SHEK VERSUS MAO TSE-TUNG

This Communist poster was issued in the aftermath of the party's win over the Nationalists. Mao's total victory was followed by a series of policies and plans which led to a great deal of suffering for the Chinese population. Once in power the Communists were able to impose the kind of grand policies that often led to famine which in turn resulted in millions of deaths. No resistance to Mao's rule was tolerated and for decades political opposition of any kind was crushed. (Philip Jowett)

IMAGES OF WAR

CHIANG KAI-SHEK VERSUS MAO TSE-TUNG

THE BATTLE FOR CHINA 1946–1949

PHILIP S . JOWETT

Pen & Sword
MILITARY

To my family

First published in Great Britain in 2018 by
Pen & Sword Military
an imprint of
Pen & Sword Books Ltd
47 Church Street
Barnsley
South Yorkshire
S70 2AS

Copyright © Pen & Sword Books 2018

ISBN 978 1 47387 484 8

The right of Philip S. Jowett to be identified as Author of this Work has been asserted by him in accordance with the Copyright, Designs and Patents Act 1988.

A CIP catalogue record for this book is available from the British Library

Typeset in 12/14 Gill Sans by
Aura Technology and Software Services, India

Printed and bound by CPI UK

Pen & Sword Books Ltd incorporates the imprints of
Pen & Sword Archaeology, Atlas, Aviation, Battleground, Discovery, Family History, History, Maritime, Military, Naval, Politics, Railways, Select, Social History, Transport, True Crime, and Claymore Press, Frontline Books, Leo Cooper, Praetorian Press, Remember When, Seaforth Publishing and Wharncliffe.

For a complete list of Pen & Sword titles please contact
Pen & Sword Books Limited
47 Church Street, Barnsley, South Yorkshire, S70 2AS, England
E-mail: enquiries@pen-and-sword.co.uk
Website: www.pen-and-sword.co.uk

Contents

Acknowledgements

My thanks go to Lennart Andersson, Gavin Goh, General Lowe Chung-yang, Kevin Mahoney, Paul V. Walsh and the many others who have helped with photographs and information over the years.

Introduction

The Chinese Civil War of 1946–9 was fought between the Nationalists under the command of Chiang Kai-shek and the Communists under Mao Tse-tung. Although the fighting began in earnest in 1946, it really started in 1945 and ended in the first weeks of 1950. Both leaders during the war symbolised the political factions that were ready to fight 'to the end' over the future of China. They were longstanding leaders of their forces, with Chiang having been in charge of the Nationalists for twenty years. Mao had been one of the leaders of the Chinese Communists since the 1920s but had taken power in the mid-1930s following the Long March. With armies totalling 7 million and some battles involving several million troops, this certainly was war on a vast scale. The ordinary people of China were to suffer, as usual, because of political differences that many did not understand or care about. As a consequence of the fighting, disease and famine, there were millions of unrecorded civilian deaths. By the time the fighting ended nearly 30 million of the Chinese population had been displaced with little hope of support from either faction. The bitter rivalry between the two opposing leaders meant that no quarter would be given regardless of the cost to the Chinese people. It was also certain that no peaceful end to the conflict was possible. As the outside world watched indifferently, the fighting was to continue until one side was vanquished and the victor could claim to have finally united China under one government.

China had been at war with itself almost continuously from the fall of the Imperial Qing Empire in 1911 to the end of the Second World War in 1945. During these thirty-four years several civil wars had been fought, usually by military groups with no political affiliations. The rise of revolutionary forces in the early twentieth century gradually changed the political outlook for China. Unfortunately for China there were two wings of the revolutionary movement, the original Kuomintang Nationalist Party, formed in the nineteenth century, and the 'New' Communist Party of China. After the death of its founder Sun Yat-sen in 1925, the Nationalist Party moved to the right while the Communists moved to the left. Conflict between the two parties was inevitable especially when any Communists who were also members of the Nationalist Party were brutally expelled in 1927. The killing of thousands of them by Nationalist death squads created a bitter hatred between the two groups. This expulsion and the resulting massacre had taken place in the middle of a military campaign by the Nationalists' National Revolutionary Army to defeat the Warlord

Armies in 1926–8. When the Nationalist-led Northern Expedition finally defeated the military groups controlling China in 1928 a new government was formed in Nanking. This Nationalist government was led by the National Revolutionary Army's military commander Chiang Kai-shek who became the national leader.

Chiang was a fervent anti-Communist and his main aim for the next fifteen years was to totally destroy the 'reds' in China. Throughout the 1930s his Nationalist Army launched a series of 'extermination' campaigns to destroy Communist bases throughout the country. These bases had been set up by the survivors of the 1927 massacres including Mao Tse-tung, who eventually became their leader in the mid-1930s. The Communists survived these attacks under the leadership of their new leader Mao who moulded them into a tough political and military force. When the Japanese invaded China in July 1937 it was debatable whether the left- and right-armed struggle would continue. Faced with the brutal and unprovoked invasion of China, an uneasy anti-Japanese alliance between the Communists and Nationalists was made in 1937. This alliance was formed after the kidnapping of Chiang Kai-shek by some of his commanders in 1936. They wanted Chiang to put off his fight with the Communists for the time being to concentrate on fighting the Japanese. He had little choice but to agree and a deal was struck which meant that Communist units would temporarily join the Nationalist Army. This 'deal with the devil' ended in violence in 1941 and from then on the two sides fought their own wars against the Japanese.

Chiang was bolstered by the outbreak of the Pacific War which overnight made him a 'valued' ally of the British and USA. From 1941 until the defeat of the Japanese in 1945 the Communists and Nationalists fought their own campaigns against the Imperial Army in China. Both Chiang and Mao now had one eye on what would happen after Japan's defeat and the renewal of the pre-1937 civil war. For most of the war the Nationalists blockaded the Communists in their bases in Northern and North-Western China. The hundreds of thousands of Nationalist troops fighting the Communists between 1937 and 1945 could have been deployed instead against the Japanese. At the same time the Communists moved their armies into new bases in Manchuria. These were to be prepared as the starting point for a post-1945 struggle with the Nationalists. When the Japanese surrendered in August 1945 it was obvious that both Chiang and Mao planned to renew their quest for power. The Nationalist Army and Communist guerrillas rushed to fill the vacuum created by the withdrawal of the Japanese. In some cases the Japanese were allowed to continue to garrison cities and towns they were in control of pre-August 1945. In the chaos that ensued in late 1945 both the Communists and Nationalists desperately tried to grab as much territory as possible. Although officially Mao and Chiang agreed to talks to try and establish a peaceful settlement, the reality was that they now prepared for war. This war would decide the fate of China and end decades of conflict but not until the nation had suffered for another five years.

Cadets at the Nationalist Central Military Academy at Chengtu go through their drill on the parade ground in the summer of 1942. After a few months of training these soldiers would be assigned to one of the elite divisions of Chiang Kai-shek's army. Chiang knew that many of his commanders were inherently disloyal and in his words had 'brittle loyalty' to his government. He hoped that he could at least rely on the troops that were trained at the better military academies such as this one. In a few years time these men would be battling their old enemy the Communists in the long and bitter Civil War. (Philip Jowett)

Boy soldiers of the Nationalist Army are seen in the final days of the Second World War in Burma in August 1945. Young soldiers like this were often attached to units as mascots but also saw action when necessary. By the time these soldiers had finished fighting in the Civil War they would still probably be in their teens. The boy on the right is carrying the unit standard while his two young comrades have been issued with Mauser rifles. (Philip Jowett)

Chiang Kai-shek, the titular leader of China, is pictured making a speech at the height of the struggle against the invading Japanese. Whatever Chiang's strengths and weaknesses, he was determined to continue to fight the Japanese even when a peace deal was a strong possibility. He shared a vehement hatred of Communists with the Japanese establishment and could have come to some accommodation with them. Instead, the Nationalists held out even after the disastrous military defeats of 1937 and 1938. Whatever Chiang thought of the Japanese, his mind was always on his other enemy who he knew he would have to face up to eventually, the Communists. (Philip Jowett)

Soldiers of the Chinese Red Army are inspected by one of their officers at their headquarters during the Sino-Japanese War. The growth of the Red Army during the 1937–45 war with Japan was strongest in Northern China and Manchuria. With the Nationalists having no real presence in these regions, the Communists' main foe was the Japanese Imperial Army. Although they did not control every part of Manchuria in August 1945, this became the main base for the political and military effort against the Nationalists. (Philip Jowett)

Two of the future leaders of the victorious Communist Army, Mao Tse-tung and Chu Teh are seen at their Yenan base in the late 1930s. It was from the relative safety of their Shensi headquarters that the Communists build up a military and political machine to take on Chiang Kai-shek. With only a hardcore of strong supporters behind him, Mao had struggled to gain power since the 1920s. Gradually and often ruthlessly he had progressed to leadership by the start of the Civil War. (Philip Jowett)

This photograph taken on the Burma Front in early 1945 shows the meeting between the Allied trained and equipped troops of the X-Force and the Y-Force. Y-Force was the Chinese Nationalist Army trained by US advisors in Yunnan province but not equipped and armed by them. His comrade with the US steel helmet and Thompson sub-machine gun has been better fed, equipped and armed by the British and Americans at their training camps in India. These better equipped soldiers of X-Force were renamed the 1st and 6th New Armies and were air-lifted by the US Air Force into China and then into Manchuria in 1946. (Philip Jowett)

In an uncomfortable meeting this Jeep is full of rival leaders from the Communist and Nationalist factions. They are meeting at the Communist base at Yenan in late 1944 as part of US attempts to broker peace between the two sides. Mao Tse-tung sits in the front seat with a US Army member of the negotiating team, while Patrick J. Hurley, the US Ambassador to China, is in the back. Hurley sits between the Communist military leader Chu Teh and the Nationalist General Ho Ying-chin. Hurley spent from September 1944 until November 1945 making earnest, but ultimately futile, attempts to try and mediate between Mao and Chiang. (Philip Jowett)

The surrender of all Japanese Imperial forces in China is accepted from General Neiji Okamura by Nationalist General Ho Ying-chin at a ceremony in the Central Military Academy in Nanking. It took place on 9 September at 9.00 am and formally ended the fourteen-year hostilities between China and Japan. Any hope of peace in China was soon ended, however, as the Communists and Nationalists geared up for a renewal of the Civil War. (Philip Jowett)

Chapter One

Unreal Peace, 1945-6

At the end of the war in China in August 1945 the two sides in the Civil War which had raged since 1927 were ready to renew hostilities. That same month Mao Tse-tung made a report to his party's 7th Party Congress in which he emphasised the strong position of the Communists at the time. He told them that there were at least 95,500,000 people living in Communist controlled areas. In regard to the army of the Communists, he said that there were 910,000 men in the regular Red Army with an additional 2,200,000 militia. Although many of the militia were unarmed, they were able to support the regulars and be converted to regulars when arms were available. On the political front Mao said that the Communist Party had 1,100,000 members who would support the Red Army. This report was like a rallying cry to all Communists in China that battle would soon be joined with the Nationalists. However, this optimistic declaration by Mao disguised some of the weaknesses of the Communist armies at the start of the war. For instance, they were particularly short of heavy weaponry in the early days of the fighting. They had been handed large numbers of guns by the defeated Japanese in August 1945 but it was reported that they only had twenty-four batteries of artillery in the regular army.

On the Nationalist side Chiang Kai-shek was confident in August 1945 that his army would soon defeat the 'disorganised' Communists. Although, for economic reasons, he had been forced to cut the Nationalist Army from 3 million to 2.6 million, he thought that it was still large enough to defeat the Communists. Not without reason, Chiang Kai-shek believed that the USA would supply him with all the necessary weaponry to destroy his political enemies. Chiang was, however, a realist and knew that the Nationalist Army had many problems which affected its performance. In an often quoted statement Chiang said that the Nationalist Army officers 'had a lack of professional skills' and that they were 'guilty of neglect and ill treatment of their men'. He bemoaned the high level of endemic corruption in the higher ranks and the lack of co-operation with other unit commanders in battle. Despite these weaknesses, the Nationalist Army in late 1945 had what appeared to be an overwhelming superiority. It was built around a thirty-nine-division-strong core of US-trained troops with several first-class formations such as the 1st and 6th New Armies. In total the army had a strength of 324 divisions and 60 or so brigades along with 89 guerrilla units of about 2,000 men each. In addition, there would soon be 1.5 million paramilitary Peace Preservation Corps recruited.

As Chiang tried to take advantage of this perceived superiority he decided, along with his US advisors, to move into Manchuria. With the assistance of the US Navy and Air Force the Nationalists had moved over 500,000 Nationalist troops into Northern China and Manchuria by October 1945. Although most were transported by ship, a large-scale air lift also moved significant numbers of troops. At the same time, 53,000 US Marines took control of the cities of Peking and Tientsin in Northern China and large parts of the province of Shantung. In the disorder in Manchuria the Communists had moved into areas previously occupied by the Japanese. To add to the confusion some towns were captured by forces described as 'free-lance' troops. These units were made up of men who it was reported had not made up their mind if they were pro-Chiang or pro-Mao.

Although officially the USA backed Chiang and his Nationalist Army, many in US government circles favoured a peaceful settlement in China. Ambassador Patrick Hurley persuaded Chiang Kai-shek to invite Mao to Chungking for talks in August. With assurances from Hurley, Mao agreed to attend the talks, which began on 28 August 1945. As the talks were underway Mao's military commander, Lin Piao, was leading a large army of 130,000 Communists into Manchuria from their wartime bases in Jehol and northern Hopeh province. When Chiang found out about the Communists' move the talks broke down and the Nationalists transferred additional troops into Manchuria. Meanwhile, Lin Piao's forces were consolidating themselves in Western Manchuria in preparation for the battle for control of the region.

The breakdown of talks led to the resignation of Hurley, who was replaced as the peacemaker by US General Marshall. Marshall tried to arrange new talks but these would have to wait until the New Year as fighting intensified in many areas of China. By early December 1945 although officially there had been a peace of sorts in China, up to 80,000 Communists and Nationalists had been killed in clashes. According to statistics published at the time, 144 Nationalist divisions with a total of 1,200,000 troops were moving against their Communist enemies.

General Cheng Tung-kuo, the commander of the New 4th Army in Burma from 1943 until 1944. He was then given the title of Deputy Commander of the Chinese Army in Burma from 1944. During the coming Civil War he was to command the 1st Army in Manchuria made up of six elite divisions. He is seen here addressing some of his troops at a parade at Nanning on 17 August 1945. (US National Archives)

Chinese Nationalist soldiers disembark from a US transport plane in Northern China as large numbers of government troops are moved into the region in the autumn of 1945. They effectively flew 'over the heads' of Communist troops who controlled much of Northern China. When troops arrived in Peking they faced no opposition from the Communists who had retired into the countryside. In many cases they took over directly from Japanese troops, who had remained in control of their garrisons to keep the Communists out. Although these soldiers are being welcomed by the locals, there were many other civilians who did not see these 'Southern' troops as liberators. Some saw these 'alien' troops as just another occupying force and simply wanted to be left alone by the Chinese government. (Philip Jowett)

Soviet troops of the Far Eastern Army which conquered the puppet state of Manchuria are seen in Harbin on the banks of the Songhua River. The Soviet invasion of Manchuria in August 1945 led to a long occupation of the region by the Red Army. Although the Nationalist Chinese government officially protested about the occupation of Manchuria by the Soviets, in some ways it suited Chiang Kai-shek. By May 1946 the Soviet Army had totally withdrawn from Manchuria but not before taking much of the moveable infrastructure with it. (Philip Jowett)

US Marines march through the streets of a South Manchurian city as they assist the Nationalists in taking control of parts of the region. They are greeted by happy Chinese civilians who were just relieved to be liberated from the hard Japanese occupation. The presence of US troops and Marines in China gave the Chinese false hope that they would bring stability to the country. In reality, the vast majority of the US troops would soon return home leaving the Communists and Nationalists to battle for control of China. (Philip Jowett)

A US Marine who is part of the force sent to support the Nationalist return to occupied territory poses outside a base with a Chinese soldier. The US Marine force, which reached a total of 50,000 men, was sent to assist in the smooth takeover of cities in Northern China and Manchuria. By 1946 this force had been reduced to about 25,000 before the majority left China in 1947. (Philip Jowett)

Two Communist fighters read a poster pasted to a wall in a Manchurian town held by the Red Army. The poster claims that the Communists support the attempts by General Marshall to broker a peace deal between them and the Nationalists. It says that the Communists will honour the 10 January 1946 truce, although the truth was that neither side was prepared to make peace. Fighting broke out in various parts of China in April 1946 and was followed by a temporary ceasefire in June. (Philip Jowett)

Communist troops wait at an airfield for the arrival of US General C. Marshall who had been tasked with the onerous job of brokering a peace between them and the Nationalists. Marshall was the former Commander-in-Chief of the US Forces in the Far East in the Second World War. It was thought that Marshall's reputation would give him the authority to deal with the slippery characters, Mao and Chiang. Neither leader was really sincere about making peace and the astute General Marshall soon came to this conclusion after discussions with both factions. (Philip Jowett)

The three main leaders of the Chinese Communists, Chou En-lai, Mao Tse-tung and Chu Teh, wait at an airport for the arrival of General Marshall on 23 December 1945. Mao was the political leader of the Communists while Chou En-lai served as his deputy and as a military commander. Chu Teh had been a Red Army commander since the late 1920s and during the Civil War he maintained his long-time role as supreme commander of the army. (Philip Jowett)

A Nationalist government Military Policeman relaxes with a book after patrolling a recently 'liberated' Northern Chinese city. The Nationalist Army and police had a difficult task in keeping law and order in cities and towns which had been occupied by the Japanese for up to eight years. In Northern China and Manchuria they were often faced by underground Communist forces who constantly challenged their authority. (US National Archives)

In the autumn of 1945 a Nationalist soldier guards a government building which flies the flags of China and the Kuomintang Party. Soldiers like this man often took over the control of Chinese cities from their enemies the Japanese Imperial Army. The Japanese had been allowed or even asked by the Nationalists to help them hold cities until they could get troops to relieve them. Even though the Nationalists and Japanese had been bitter rivals, the anti-Communist sympathies of the Imperial Army meant they would rather hand over power to Chiang Kai-shek than Mao. (Philip Jowett)

A Nakajima KI-84 ex-Japanese fighter has its engine fired up before going on a flight after its recent capture by the Nationalists. This was one of the most modern types in service with the Japanese and a few were used by the Nationalist Air Force in the early stages of the Civil War. It is probable that a few Japanese mercenary pilots were employed by the Nationalists during the Civil War. In March 1946 it was reported that a number of Japanese had also joined the Nationalist Army in various roles. (Philip Jowett)

Two Kawasaki KI-48 bombers formerly in service with the Japanese Imperial Air Force are lined up at a Nationalist airfield at the start of the Civil War. The number of Japanese aircraft serving with the Nationalist Air Force was small but they were the main source of planes in 1945. It is not certain if Japanese air crew flew these planes but it would make sense when their compatriots often crewed ex-Imperial Army tanks. (Philip Jowett)

These militiamen photographed in 1945 were the backbone of the Communist forces in the early days of the Civil War. They are armed with a mixture of home-made muskets and a single Thompson sub-machine gun. The Thompson is one of those made in the Taiyuan arsenal of the Shansi Warlord Yen Hsi-shan. When the ammunition for these guns ran out they were handed from the regular Communist forces to these guerrillas. When modern arms were acquired by the Communists these part-time soldiers would be transferred to regular units. (Philip Jowett)

Chapter Two

The Fighting Begins, 1946

In 1946 civil war seemed inevitable as both sides talked openly about conflict. There was still another round of peace talks to go though, beginning in January 1946 with Chungking the venue. This time the talks were led by Chou En-lai for the Communists and Nationalist General Chang Chih-chung. A ceasefire agreement was duly signed between the two sides on 10 January 1946. One of the main criteria of the agreement was the call for the unification of the Communist and Nationalist armies into one force. Once both armies were reorganised a 'unified' Chinese Army of between fifty and sixty divisions would be formed. This would be a politically 'neutral' army which would contain units from both army's personnel. Of course, this was a non-starter and both the Communists and Nationalists chose to ignore it. Although lip service was paid to the agreement, neither side really intended to honour it no matter how much they said they did.

Chiang Kai-shek had, he believed, the upper hand in China in early 1946 and was at the height of his powers. He still had the prestige as one of the Allied leaders against Japan and had the loyalty of most of his powerful army's officers. Chiang's Nationalist Army in early 1946 had a strength of 2,500,000, which were formed into 278 brigades. Brigades and divisions in the Nationalist Army both had an average strength of 10,000 men as their organisation was very loose. A Nationalist division was only 66 per cent the strength of a Second World War US Infantry division and had only 33 per cent the artillery of the US equivalent.

By late 1945 the first-line strength of the Nationalist Air Force was 350 aircraft but there were another 650 planes stored for future use. The shortage of air crew meant that it was pointless having more aircraft without the personnel to fly them. Other reports said that its strength was 500 aircraft formed into 5 fighter and 3 bomber groups and 1 reconnaissance squadron along with 2 transport groups. All the planes apart from a few British Mosquitoes were of US Second World War vintage and were adequate with no air opposition from the Communists. By April 1947 there were only 318 planes in service out of 415 listed as available and despite US assistance this total had fallen 3 months later to 277.

The Chinese Nationalist Navy was small but relatively efficient, and was helped by the fact that it had no Communist equivalent to counter it. It was made up mainly of lighter vessels and 131 landing craft with its largest ship being the British cruiser the ex-HMS *Aurora*. A training school was also established by the US at the port of Tsingtao to train ratings and officers to expand the navy.

This powerful army, navy and air force was now to be turned on the Communist Army, especially in Manchuria. In 1946 the Communist forces totalled 1,278,000 both men and women and these were reorganised in May into 6 field armies. They were organised into 3 brigade or division columns which had strengths of between 12,000 and 21,000 men. As the war progressed the brigades were expanded to divisional size, thus increasing the number of columns with a higher total of combatants. In July 1946 there were still 84,000 Japanese prisoners of war and 4,100 Koreans in Northern China. Many of these were to be employed by the Communists in roles such as tank drivers, artillerymen and other support roles. The Communist Army was still in a stage of development in 1946 and was to continue to expand until its final victory in 1949.

In early 1946 the Nationalist Army moved into Manchuria in strength with its armies succeeding in moving northwards from their bases in the south-west of the region. By March they had captured Mukden but any further advance towards the city of Changchun was halted by heavy Communist resistance. In mid-April Changchun fell to the Communists but they only managed to hold on to it for a month, regaining it again on 22 May after a major campaign. The Nationalists went onto the offensive during May and pushed the Communists back towards their bases north of the Sungari River. They advanced towards the Communist base at Harbin and the city would have fallen if a ceasefire had not be arranged at the insistence of the USA. On 10 June the ceasefire was declared in Manchuria, but it had collapsed by the 26th of the month and substantial fighting resumed. By early May 1946 the Communists claimed to control 70 per cent of Manchuria, which if by this they meant territory, they were correct. Nearly all the major cities however were strongly held by the Nationalists and at least for the time being were impregnable to Communist attack. In May they also captured the northern Manchurian city of Harbin, which was taken on the orders of Mao Tse-tung to give the Communists an urban base in the region. By the autumn of 1946 the Communists controlled most of the countryside of Manchuria and a few urban areas in the North. The Nationalists controlled most of Central and Southern Manchuria and spent most of 1946 digging trenches and avoiding fighting in the field against the Communists. This meant that they lost the initiative in many parts of the country and left the areas around the garrisons to be exploited by the 500,000-strong Communist Army. For the remainder of 1946 the Nationalist Army went on the defensive in Manchuria and were content to hold on to what they had.

Two senior Japanese Imperial Army officers being executed by smartly uniformed Nationalist Military Policemen in the summer of 1946. War crimes trials took place in China at which Japanese officers who had commanded in occupied areas between 1937 and 1945 were tried. The ordinary Japanese soldier was usually allowed to leave China without punishment as their officers took responsibility for their brutal treatment of the population. A large crowd has gathered to watch justice be meted out to these officers whose names and crimes are not recorded by the photographer. One of the most popular of these executions took place on 10 March 1947 when the officer largely responsible for the Nanking Massacre in 1937 was shot. (Philip Jowett)

Chiang Kai-shek making a speech in front of the mausoleum of his mentor, Sun Yat-sen, in Nanking on 5 May 1946. He announced the return of the Nationalist capital to the city which was meant to reaffirm his government's control of the country. By Chiang's side as usual is his wife, Madame Chiang, who had been an extremely strong influence on her husband during the Second World War. She continued in this vein until the day he died, twenty-five years after the end of the Civil War. (Philip Jowett)

A 12-year-old boy soldier of the 22nd Nationalist Division stands guard over the personal effects of his comrades. He is wearing a toned down version of the adult uniform worn with a captured Japanese Imperial Army winter hat. Although boy soldiers had been common in the Chinese Army previously, by 1946 they were less so. (US National Archives)

Troops of the 52nd Nationalist Division of the New 6th Army which were stationed in Shanghai are being moved from the port of Chinwangtao to Manchuria. Chiang Kai-shek's policy of keeping control over Manchuria where the Communists had a strong foothold was a strategic mistake. These troops are waiting to embark on one of the landing ships sent by the US Navy to move thousands of them northwards. Although these soldiers look fit and well, a number of Nationalist troops sent to Manchuria were unfit and had ulcers, VD, dysentery and cholera. A large number of troops were reported to have died from cholera while being transported to the North. (US National Archives)

Soldiers of the 52nd Nationalist Division of the New 6th Army climb the gangplank onto their transports which will sail them up the Chinese coast to Manchuria. In early 1946 a 241,500-strong Nationalist force was waiting in Northern China to be moved into Manchuria. This force included the US-trained New 1st and New 6th Armies, the 13th Armoured Army and the 92nd 'Airborne' Army with two divisions. The official divisional strength of the Nationalist Army in 1946 was 14,000 men, but most had 11,000 or less. (US National Archives)

Above: Girl students from Nanking University take part in a government organised demonstration in the summer of 1946. They are part of a mass meeting which called for the war against the Communists to be prosecuted. Although some fervent Nationalist supporters did exist at this time, many were obliged to take part in demonstrations like this under pressure from the authorities. (Philip Jowett)

Opposite above: These Nationalist troops moving from Central China to Manchuria are about to get on their transport ships. They are each carrying a bundle of four Mauser rifles with bayonets fixed to give to their comrades when they land. Most of these troops would end up encircled in the various garrison towns of Manchuria surrounded by their Communist foes. (US National Archives)

Opposite below: Young nurses attached to the 52nd Nationalist Division wait to board their transport ships in 1946. Even the better Chinese units, such as the 22nd, would have had only the most rudimentary of medical services. These nurses wear the same light khaki uniforms as their male colleagues and only the first-aid boxes they sit on distinguish them as medical workers. (US National Archives)

Nationalist troops march into Mukden, the main industrial city in Manchuria, to take positions being left by the Soviet Army on 11 March 1946. At the same time Communist forces were arriving from the North from their guerrilla bases in that part of Manchuria. In this land grab both the Nationalists and the Communists tried to gain as much territory as possible before a ceasefire came into place. Note that not all of these troops are armed showing the shortages of armaments that still existed in 1946 in both opposing armies. Chiang Kai-shek was not impressed by the quality of many of his soldiers even in 1946 and was quoted as saying, 'The soldier's combat skills are so poor that they cannot fight!' (Philip Jowett)

In early March 1946 armed police of the Nationalist authorities in Mukden stand guard over their city centre station. At this time the Soviet Army was in the process of leaving the city having occupied it since the previous August. The Nationalist police were really an extension of the armed forces and were as heavily armed as their army colleagues. There was a great deal of tension in the city and, as the caption to this photograph says, it was filled with 'fear and dread'. (Philip Jowett)

A Nationalist soldier inspects a factory recently abandoned by the Soviet Army in Mukden in Manchuria in early March 1946. The Russians stripped most of the factories and workshops in Mukden and transported their machinery back to the Soviet Union. The soldier is staring at the hole blasted in the factory's wall to allow the heavy machinery to be moved out more easily. His uniform appears to have been taken from Japanese Imperial Army stores, although the Chinese did produce similar winter clothing. (Philip Jowett)

Above: Two young sentries stand in front of their sandbagged guard post outside the Kuomintang Party Headquarters in Mukden in mid-March 1946. Above them is a portrait of the Nationalist leader Chiang Kai-shek and a banner with a suitable anti-Communist theme. At this time fighting had begun in the major Manchurian city to gain control after it had recently been abandoned by the Soviet Army. In all of the almost twenty years of Chiang's reign as leader of Nationalist China he had never really controlled Manchuria. He had ruled the region through the Manchurian warlord, Marshal Chang Hsueh-liang, for a few years before the Japanese invasion in 1931. (Philip Jowett)

Opposite above: Communist militia men line up for the camera in the early stages of the war in Manchuria in 1946. These young fighters would have grown up in the 1937–45 period fighting with their fathers in the expanding Communist guerrilla armies. The large number of militia in Manchuria allowed the Communist regular army to expand rapidly when weaponry became available. They are armed with a number of types of rifle with at least one Arisaka Type 98 Japanese rifle among them. (Philip Jowett)

Opposite below: In the early stages of the Civil War a squad of Communist troops are photographed outside their headquarters. Most the men are armed with the US UDM-42 sub-machine guns which were supplied to the Communists by the US Office of Strategic Services in the closing months of the Second World War. When the Communist guerrillas were fighting the Japanese they were regarded as an ally of the USA and got limited military aid from them. At this stage the Communists were short of weaponry and would have been pleased to use these guns despite a shortage of ammunition for them. (Philip Jowett)

Above: This artillery outpost of the Nationalist Army is situated on the outskirts of a village in Northern Kiangsu during fighting in late September 1946. At this time the Nationalists lines of communication in the region were under threat by the Communists. Their light artillery piece is probably an ex-Japanese infantry gun, many of which were captured by them in 1945. The men are all wearing the new type US-style uniform along with the ex-US Army peaked cap. (Philip Jowett)

Opposite above: Two of the prominent Nationalist generals are pictured on their way to a military conference in Japan in July 1946. They are General Ho Ying-chin on the left and General Chin Teh-chun on the right of the picture. Ho was the former Chief of Staff of the Nationalist Army and Chin was Vice Commander of the National Defence Ministry. (Philip Jowett)

Opposite below: In Northern Kiangsu province in late September 1946 trucks of the Nationalist Army provided by the USA are preparing to take machine-gun ammunition to the front line. Trucks like this were supplied in large numbers as part of US aid in the early stages of the Civil War. As the war developed US-supplied equipment and weaponry found its way by one means or another into the hands of the Communists. (Philip Jowett)

Above: A train is about to leave Tientsin railway station fit to burst with civilians travelling to the Manchurian city of Chinchow in March 1946. Because there is no room on the train some are fastening their baggage to the underneath of the carriage. The railway network kept the various Nationalist strongholds connected with each other despite repeated Communist guerrilla attacks. (Philip Jowett)

Opposite above: Off-duty Communist troops attempt to win the 'hearts and minds' campaign by helping build roads in the summer of 1946. Mao Tse-tung well understood the propaganda benefits of his troops doing public works like this for the local population where they were operating. The other side of the Communist policy to the civilian population was the punishment of any who co-operated with the Nationalists. (Philip Jowett)

Opposite below: Nationalist troops of the 94th Corps are given machine-gun training with ZB-26 light machine guns in 1946. These machine guns are a 1930s model but have come fresh from the arsenal which is still producing this model. Although the size of the Nationalist Army was officially reduced after 1945, the level of desertions meant new recruits were needed. (Philip Jowett)

These heavy machine-gunners of the 94th Corps are training with Browning M1919 machine guns in the summer of 1946. The old problem of too many types of weapons in service with the Chinese Army continued into the Civil War period. Although large numbers of US small arms were supplied to the Nationalists after 1945, they still relied to a large extent on earlier weaponry. Much of this was manufactured in local government arsenals still under the control of commanders who continued to act largely independently of the central government. (Philip Jowett)

Nationalist machine-gunners fire their Type 3 medium machine gun behind an earthwork in the early fighting in China. The Nationalists captured large amounts of Japanese armaments in August 1945 and used them alongside their US-supplied armaments. The Type 3 was the oldest type of Japanese-produced machine gun in service with the Imperial Army. This type would have been in limited service with the Nationalists until they could get modern machine guns from the USA and Canada. (Philip Jowett)

Mao Tse-tung is pictured at the time of the early Civil War when his dreams of taking control of China were beginning to become a reality. In 1946 Mao had held long discussions with Lin Piao over the Communists' military strategy going forward. These talks set in place the tactics and strategies which were eventually to give the People's Army its final victory. (Philip Jowett)

Chapter Three

Nationalist Accendancy, 1947

Looking from the outside the Civil War appeared to be going the Nationalist way at the start of 1947. The Nationalists had, according to their records, 3,700,000 troops but the US intelligence reports said they had 1 million men less. Nationalist forces in 1947 had more rifles, more artillery and the only viable air force and navy. In reality there were many weaknesses in the Nationalist Army which would eventually lead to its defeat. In 1946 decisions were made, especially in Manchuria, which would eventually lead to their final defeat.

In early 1947 the Nationalists were beginning to lose ground in Manchuria and were bogged down in other parts of China. Chiang Kai-shek was looking for a victory to bolster his cause which he admitted was losing its momentum. He received a proposal from General Hu Tsung-nan that it would be possible to launch an offensive to take the Communist base at Yenan in Shensi province. Hu's plan was to drive the Communists out of their main political base in the North and disrupt the administration of their war effort. It had to be kept secret and for once it appeared that it had been kept from even some high-ranking officers. There were 150,000 troops and 75 aircraft committed to the operation, which was the largest formation used in the Civil War up to that date. Hu wanted more troops to be sent from the South but Chiang refused and the offensive began on 12 March. Some Nationalist forces were sent on a diversionary operation to the west of Yenan, while the main force headed straight for it. This main force, which moved out on 14 March, was made up of the 1st and 29th Armies and was confronted by 20,000 Communist troops under the command of P'eng Teh-huai. They put up a fierce resistance while the Communists made a hasty withdrawal from Yenan which fell on 19 March to the 1st Army. The fall of Yenan was trumpeted in the Nationalist press and worldwide as a major victory but the significance of this was overplayed. In reality the Communists had other plans for the coming year and were pragmatic about the loss of their long-term base.

The Nationalists now spent most of 1947 strengthening their fortified positions throughout China and building up their garrisons. They rarely ventured out of these outposts to attack the Communists in the countryside around them. The fortified towns and cities soon attracted more refugees from Communist rule which widened their perimeter. To defend these Nationalist held towns and cities required more troops which only increased the number of mouths to feed. Although in the short-term these garrisons and the people sheltering in them felt safe they were becoming increasingly isolated. The Nationalist soldiers in these garrisons spent most of their time in barracks and even among the higher quality troops there was low morale. Even though the numbers of Nationalist troops was kept up by recruiting, their losses had been horrendous. In the 17-month period between July 1946 and November 1947 it was reported that a staggering 1,690,000 Nationalist troops had been put out of action. This total was made up of 640,000 killed and 1,050,000 captured, of which a large number would have joined the Communist forces. Even though the Nationalists appeared to still be winning the war there were many weaknesses in its army. One unit, the 96th Army, seen on parade in June 1947 was reported to have only half of its men properly armed. As far as uniforms went most were fairly well clothed but only about 1 in 50 of the men were wearing steel helmets.

Enthusiastic soldiers of one of the Nationalists' youth divisions cheer their leader Chiang Kai-shek in Shanghai in early 1947. At this time the Nationalists still had high hopes of a final victory against the Communists and these young troops mirror Chiang's confidence. Youth divisions were formed almost exclusively from university and college students who were loyal to the Nationalist cause. All the troops have been issued with ex-Japanese M32 steel helmets and wear US-donated high-leg boots. (Philip Jowett)

Departing members of a US Truce Team prepare to board a C-47 on 27 February 1947. They have been working in the city of Hsinhsiang in North Honan province as part of Truce Team # 10. Some of the city's garrison wearing their newly issued 1947 model uniforms parade in their honour at the air base. All US attempts to broker local and national truces was constantly frustrated by both the Communists and Nationalists desire to continue the war. (Philip Jowett)

Pictured in 1947 just before the fall of Yenan in a Nationalist offensive, these men belong to the Communist guard force at Mao Tse-tung's HQ in the 'Red Capital'. When Mao and his retinue left Yenan ahead of the Nationalist attack some of his best troops were left behind to fight a rear guard action. The Communist leader was pragmatic about the loss of Yenan realising that this setback would not affect the war unduly. (Philip Jowett)

Chiang Kai-shek visits the former Communist capital of China, Yenan in Shensi province, which had fallen to the Nationalists in March 1947. Although this Nationalist victory was largely 'symbolic', it was still materially a costly defeat for the Communists. Mao put a positive spin on the fall of his long-term headquarters since the mid-1930s by saying, 'We will give Chiang Yenan, he will give us China!' By the time the Nationalists were forced to withdraw in 1948 the temporary occupation of Yenan had cost them over 100,000 casualties. (Philip Jowett)

Nationalist artillery equipped with early twentieth-century medium field guns are seen advancing on the Communist headquarters at Yenan in Shensi province in 1947. Substantial forces were committed by the Nationalists to the offensive against the base at Yenan. The number of divisions sent against Yenan were really out of proportion to the benefit of capturing the near deserted base. (Philip Jowett)

Above: Civilians left behind in Yenan when the Communist leadership and their military forces escaped from their headquarters in 1947 look worried about their fate. Any non-military left behind in Yenan could expect little help from the victorious Nationalists when they took the city. The reality was that as pro-Communists in the eyes of the Nationalists these women and old men could expect no mercy. (Philip Jowett)

Opposite: A young Nationalist soldier of the army of the Shansi warlord Yen Hsi-shan stands with the wall of his fortified garrison in the distance in April 1947. This garrison was situated close to the Shansi leader's embattled capital at Taiyuan which was under threat by Communist forces. Throughout the Civil War Yen was mainly concerned with trying to push the Communists out of the province he had controlled for about thirty years. By 1948 Yen had seven divisions in his enclave around the provincial capital at Taiyuan but one division went over to the Communists on 20 July. It was reported that by 1948 the only truly reliable division in his army was made up of Japanese who had gone over to Yen in August 1945. (Philip Jowett)

An ex-Japanese Type 94 tankette drives down the streets of Taiyuan, the provincial capital of Shansi, in 1947. This type of armoured vehicle was practically obsolete in 1939 so was of little combat use during the Civil War. Regardless of its thin armour and poor armaments, the Type 94 was widely used by both the Nationalists and the Communists. Yen Hsi-shan was grateful for any equipment he could get during the Civil War. He had to produce small arms and his own artillery in his Taiyuan arsenal because he struggled to import modern arms from abroad. (Philip Jowett)

A Nationalist sentry stands guard on the wall of his unit's garrison in Chahar province in the spring of 1947. He is part of the armies under the control of General Fu Tso-yi who was responsible for most of Northern China. It looks as if he has sustained a facial injury which has had a bandage applied, probably by one of his comrades. The Nationalist medical services were basic to say the least and more remote garrisons like this would have been fortunate to have a doctor attached to them. (Philip Jowett)

These soldiers from a Chahar provincial garrison march through town using a camel to carry their kit and other equipment in 1947. They are stationed on the edge of the Gobi Desert and camels were often the only draught animals available to both armies in the region. Away from the main war fronts in the far north of China the Nationalist Army often had little opposition until the end of the Civil War in 1949. (Philip Jowett)

Machine-gunners from a garrison in Chahar province practise in the desert outside their headquarters. They are armed with a Type 24 water cooled heavy machine gun which is a Chinese-produced copy of the Maxim M1908. The crew are all wearing the new type of padded cotton winter uniforms with ear flaps worn tied up on the head. In the background another member of the machine-gun crew waits with spare boxes of ammunition. In December 1947 the Nationalists were feeling the 'pinch' because of their shortage of ammunition. They had twenty-two days' supply of the 7.92mm rounds used by the Type 24 and thirty-three days' supply of the .30 rounds used in US-supplied rifles. (Philip Jowett)

Above: Nationalist troops are transported on river steamer up the Upper Yangtze River as they are moved to another garrison. The steamer was designed to carry 200 paying passengers but there are 1,800 soldiers with 50 horses on board. Both sides used the rivers of China to transport their troops from one battlefield to another. These men are sunning themselves to escape from the cramped conditions below deck. (Philip Jowett)

Opposite: The officer of a Nationalist artillery unit in Chahar province in 1947 uses a range finder during a training session. Although large numbers of US artillery pieces were supplied after 1945, these were concentrated in the hands of units in Central and Northern China. In the more remote regions of Nationalist held China most artillery was of the German and Soviet supplied types from the late 1930s. (Philip Jowett)

Above: A Nationalist supply column moves up to the front line in 1947 carrying boxes of ammunition for their comrades. Although the Nationalists had been supplied with a large number of soft-skin vehicles by the USA, draught animals were still important to them. These troops appear to belong to one of the more disciplined formations of the Nationalist Army. Chiang's better troops seem to have been issued with war booty Japanese helmets at least during the first years of the Civil War. In July 1947 the US arms embargo was lifted against the Nationalist government and they immediately imported 130 million rounds of 7.92mm ammunition. This was used for the army's Mauser 98k rifles and Type 24 water cooled machine guns, which were short of ammunition by this time. (Philip Jowett)

Opposite above: Chinese mechanics check the engine of a Stearman PT-17 Kaydet trainer, which was the main training aircraft in the Nationalist Air Force. By September 1948 there were 90 PT-17s in service as the USA tried to help the Nationalists to produce enough pilots to fly their bombers and fighters. Air superiority was one of the advantages that the Nationalists had over the Communists until the latter stages of the war. It was reported that up to 700 aircraft had been transferred from stores in India to the Nationalists. A high attrition rate meant that many of these planes had to be cannibalised to keep a smaller number operational. (Lennart Andersson)

Opposite below: The pilot of a Canadian supplied DH Mosquito attack bomber of the Nationalist Air Force smiles for the camera in front of his plane. These aircraft were the only new types that were not supplied by the USA to the Nationalists after 1945. A contract for 200 of these planes was signed by China and Canada in 1947 and a large number participated in the war. Part of the deal was for a Canadian training team to work in China to prepare Chinese pilots to fly the aircraft. (Philip Jowett)

A Nationalist fighter unit equipped with USA-supplied Mustang P-51B fighters discuss their next mission against the People's Liberation Army. The P-51 was the mainstay of the Nationalist fighter force during the Civil War but there were too few available to affect the result of the conflict. This type of aircraft was used as a fighter bomber on most missions as it had no fighter opposition from the Communists until near the end of the war. (Cody Images)

An elderly Tupolev SB-2 light bomber supplied by the Soviet Union in the late 1930s is still in service with the Nationalists in 1947. Most planes in the Nationalist inventory were newer US types but any surviving aircraft from the 1930s and the Second World War would also be used. There was a high attrition rate among all Nationalist war planes in the 1930s and 1940s so this SB-2 was a rarity during the Civil War. The Nationalist Air Force was largely inactive during the Communist Winter offensive of 1947–8 when severe and icy winds stopped planes like this from operating. (Philip Jowett)

The crew of an ex-Japanese Kawasaki Ki-48 medium bomber stands in front of their plane before going on a bombing mission. The Nationalist Air Force utilised a number of the more modern of the captured Japanese planes during the Civil War. These would have been harder to keep in the air as the war progressed and many were taken out of service after 1946. According to the original caption, General Lowe Chung-yang is the man in the centre of the group inspecting this aircraft, which is part of the 6th Group. (Courtesy of General Lowe Chung-yang)

The commander of the Nationalist Air Force, General Chou Chih-ju, is pictured in 1947 when his pilots had full mastery of the air over China. Despite the odd Nationalist pilot going over to the Communists, it was not until the end of the war that they had a properly organised People's Liberation Air Force. This was made up of 6 bombers, 9 attack bombers, 9 fighters and 9 transport planes, all flown to Communist lines by deserting Nationalist pilots. The performance of the Nationalist Air Force was mixed to say the least with reports in 1947 of pilots flying around aimlessly without attempting to reach their target. (Philip Jowett)

Above: Two Communist prisoners of war read through Nationalist propaganda texts, as instructed by their captors. The political differences between the Communists and Nationalists should have made it difficult to accept former enemies into their ranks. As the war wore on it was the Communists who increasingly took former Nationalists into their army. Generally, conditions in the People's Liberation Army were superior to those in the Nationalist Army and many swapped sides happily when the opportunity arose. (US National Archives)

Opposite above: Nationalist naval ratings are parading as they receive their graduation certificates at the end of their US-run course in 1947. The navy was a small but relatively well-run force and maintained a high level of morale for the duration of the war. These trainees would soon join the crews of the Nationalist fleet of gunboats and other vessels. Most naval actions were in support of the Nationalist Army fighting along the Chinese coastline. (Philip Jowett)

Opposite below: Ex-Communist soldiers who have been sent to a re-education camp by the Nationalists march out of their barracks in 1947. The prisoners have been issued with Nationalist uniforms and are expected to join the ranks of their captors. Many of these men would desert the Nationalist Army at the first opportunity but may not have received a welcome from the Communists. During 1947 as gaps in the Nationalist ranks appeared in Manchuria volunteers did not come forward. New recruits had increasingly to be press-ganged and many did not receive sufficient training. Shortages of weaponry was now becoming an issue with some 14,000-strong divisions only having 3,000 rifles for their men! (US National Archives)

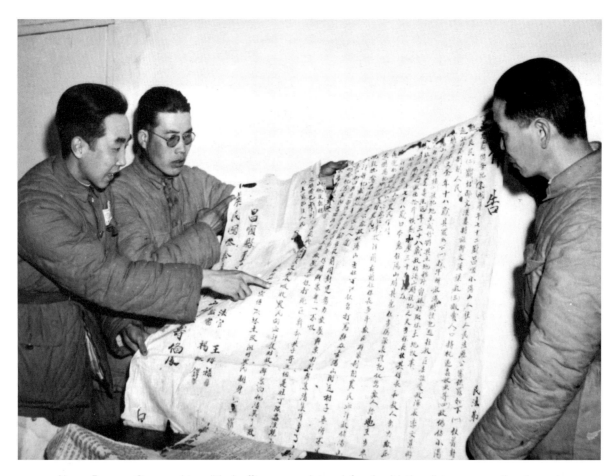

Above: Former Communist political officers are pictured for the Nationalist press reading through their propaganda material. In the first few years of the Civil War there were defections from the Communists to the Nationalists. These defections not surprisingly became less common as the war went on and the Communists began to gain the advantage. (US National Archives)

Opposite above: A Nationalist general inspects local paramilitary volunteers of the Peace Preservation Corps in 1947. The Peace Preservation Corps was a second-line force which was raised at a provincial level to support the regular Nationalist Army. Armed with older weapons, the Peace Preservation Corps suffered from poor morale and was seen as an easy target by the Communists. They targeted the Peace Preservation Corps as a source of weaponry and before their main victories against the Nationalists they captured thousands of rifles from it in local skirmishes and battles. (Philip Jowett)

Opposite below: Japanese prisoners of the Nationalists are shown to the news cameras to prove that the Communists were using these mercenaries to fight for them. In reality most Japanese who fought for both the Red Army and the Nationalist Army did so under duress. Although the vast majority of Imperial Army personnel were repatriated back to Japan, some were captured in August 1945 in isolated garrisons. Some of these troops were then given little choice but to crew captured tanks or man ex-Japanese artillery for the combatants. (Philip Jowett)

李司令检查打匪武装情形

Chapter Four

The Cockpit of Asia, Manchuria, 1947

It soon became apparent to everyone both inside and outside China that the Chinese Civil War would be largely decided in the campaigns in Manchuria. By choosing to send some of his best troops into the northern region, Chiang had thrown down the gauntlet to the Communists. At the start of 1947 Lin Piao's Communist forces in Manchuria were ready to go on to the offensive and crossed the Sungari River from the North of the region. Beginning in January the Communists launched a series of four major offensives, the second commencing in February, the third in March and the fourth in May. These offensives were largely aimed at isolating the cities of Changchun and Kirin. The final offensive in May was for the most part successful in achieving this aim, the two cities being surrounded by a total of 270,000 Communists. Although the Nationalists were able to push the Communists back across the Sungari River during the early fighting, their garrisons were gradually surrounded. As the Nationalists dug in deeper in the positions they held their troops were beginning to lose their fighting spirit. The Communists had suffered heavy losses but had gained a strong presence in most of Manchuria especially in the countryside. For the time being the Communists were not strong enough to defeat the Nationalists but were playing the long game.

Major strategic mistakes were now made by the Nationalists which were to play into the Communists hands in Manchuria. One of their worst errors was to spilt up their better units and disperse them among other less reliable units. Wasting of elite Nationalist forces by diluting them in this way only succeeded in destroying the fighting ability of the better troops. The worst examples of this policy involved the New 1st and New 6th Armies. The US-trained New 1st Army was split up with one division stationed in Mukden, one in Changchun and one in Szepinghai. Each division was reinforced by two newly formed divisions made up of largely untrained recruits, with the intention that these fresh troops would learn from their better trained comrades. In addition, the New 6th Army was also split into three smaller divisional sized units which were again reinforced with fresh recruits. Although the aim was to create larger versions of the 1st and

6th Armies the reality was it just 'diluted' the quality of the original armies. The fall in the quality of many Nationalist units meant that they were increasingly on the defensive in Manchuria.

By the summer of 1947 the Nationalists had withdrawn from many outlying parts of Manchuria. Their armies still held the cities of Changchun, Kirin, Mukden, Szepingkai and Fushun. These cities had garrisons that made up the majority of Nationalist troops in Manchuria, while the rest were holding strongpoints along the lines of communication. The situation in Nationalist cities and garrisons was shown by the plight of Mukden that summer. As one correspondent said, the garrison was 'cowering' behind its defences and hardly ever ventured from the city. Mukden's defences were poorly prepared with badly sited trenches and bunkers made out of mud which disintegrated when hit by the first shell. There was also a desperate shortage of barbed wire available to defend the defensive positions. Communist guerrillas were also increasingly active in destroying Nationalist supply lines with the assistance of local sympathisers. By 1947 the total amount of rail tracks torn up by Communist saboteurs was 10,000 miles. This left many Nationalist garrisons isolated as virtual well-armed prison camps which could be outflanked by the mobile Communist forces in Manchuria.

The Communists under the command of Lin Piao now totalled between 250,000 and 300,000 men in Manchuria, organised into 25 divisions. By this stage in the war the People's Liberation Army had also acquired large numbers of 75mm, 105mm and 155mm artillery pieces, mostly ex-Japanese types. They were also beginning to capture large numbers of Nationalist guns, many of which were also ex-Japanese war booty items. They faced the still strong Nationalist forces which were, however, now mainly garrisoning the cities it still controlled. Another Communist offensive was launched in September in Northern China and South-Western Manchuria. Its gains were lost after a strong Nationalist offensive which re-opened the communication lines broken by the PLA attack. As 1947 ended the situation in Manchuria was at a stalemate which was to be broken the following year.

Above: An infantry squad of Nationalist troops defends a roughly prepared trench on the Sungari River Front in Manchuria in 1947. These soldiers have been well armed by US aid with a Thompson sub-machine gun and P-17 rifles. On their US-supplied M2 steel helmets the troops have the white sun on a blue background decal of the Nationalist Army. The level of equipment in the Nationalist Army varied from unit to unit but as always in China, the most loyal troops received the best kit and weapons. (Gavin Goh)

Opposite above: During the winter of 1946–7 two Communist machine-gunners eat their rations at their posts ready for a Nationalist attack. At this time the Communists were struggling to maintain their positions in Manchuria against a strong and aggressive Nationalist Army. Early attempts by their forces to expand out of the Northern Manchurian base were thrown back and their leadership had to learn hard lessons. The machine gun is a Japanese Type 96 which would have been a welcome addition to the Communist armouries. (Philip Jowett)

Opposite below: Soldiers of the People's Liberation Army take a meal break during fighting in Manchuria in the winter of 1947. The troops are wearing the same basic winter uniform as their Nationalist adversaries but have removed the white sun on blue sky cap badge. By this date although the fighting in Manchuria was still in the balance, the advantage had already shifted towards the Communists. (Philip Jowett)

Above: In early 1947 Nationalist General Hsing Min outlines his plan for the defence of a Manchurian outpost to some of his officers by using a sandbox model to help him illustrate it. It was unusual for officers in the Nationalist Army to be so 'hands on' with their men but those who had been trained in Burma were often more enlightened. Unfortunately, the vast majority of the officer class of the Nationalist Army were 'old school' who kept their junior officers at arm's length. (Philip Jowett)

Opposite above: General Ma Chan-shan, the commander of the Manchurian Security Command, makes a speech to the people of Mukden on 18 April 1947. General Ma had fought the Japanese in Manchuria in 1931 and gained international celebrity status for his resistance. By 1947 Ma was an old man who now faced resistance from the kind of forces he had commanded fifteen years before. (Philip Jowett)

Opposite below: A Nationalist officer leads his unit up a road in Manchuria in the summer of 1947 with crops growing in the fields around them. They are part of a column which is on an anti-guerrilla operation in an effort to stop the advance of the Communists. It was an unusual sight to see a Nationalist unit out in the field during the Manchurian Campaign. As the Communist grip on the Manchurian countryside strengthened, units like this would be confined to their garrison. In the rear of the column is another infantry unit with its officer riding ahead of them on horseback. (Philip Jowett)

A father and son pose proudly for the Communist propaganda cameraman during a lull in the fighting in Manchuria in 1947. Only the elder soldier is armed and the son may be acting as the support soldier for his father. The Communists had developed good propaganda techniques which surpassed anything the Nationalists attempted during the war. Like most revolutionary movements, the Communists promoted war heroes who were feted in the press and later on film and in posters. (Philip Jowett)

In a show of force by the Red Army these Communist troops in Manchuria fire their ex-Japanese 50mm grenade launchers. The Communists used a large amount of war booty equipment and weaponry which was vital to their war effort, especially in the early stages of the war. Some of this Japanese weaponry had been captured by the Communists but the vast majority of it was handed over to them in 1946 by the Soviets in Manchuria. (Philip Jowett)

A Nationalist soldier guards a railway bridge over a Manchurian river in the summer of 1947. He is watching as US troops are transported by rail to embarkation ports as the majority of their forces are being withdrawn from Manchuria. As the US forces departed they left some stores for the Nationalist Army to use and this soldier's peaked cap has probably come from this source. (US National Archives)

Two People's Liberation Army propaganda officers in Manchuria use a megaphone to call for the Nationalist troops opposing them to surrender. With the Nationalist held towns and cities often surrounded by the Communists by the end of 1947 increasingly their call did not fall on 'deaf ears'. Often whole divisions and even armies began to go over to the Communists, often led by their commanding officers. (Cody Images)

Refugees from the battle for the city of Szuping in Manchuria rest on their escape from the war zone in early 1947. It was often a difficult choice for civilians during the fighting in Manchuria when they were frequently caught between the two warring factions. In many cases it was a choice between staying in an often besieged and increasingly hungry Nationalist city and leaving to an uncertain future under Communist control. There was famine in most Manchurian cities and towns and when food was available it was usually priced at 'famine' rate. Life was very difficult for most ordinary Chinese who just wanted to be ruled by a stable government which was not riddled with corruption and at least fed them in times of crisis. (Philip Jowett)

A unit of the People's Liberation Army in Manchuria moves to the front line during the fighting in Manchuria. They are all part of one of the Korean units that fought on the Communist side in the Civil War. In total there were a reported 30,000–40,000 of these 'foreign' volunteers, many of whom had joined the Red Army in Manchuria in the 1930s. The Nationalists claimed that there were 100,000 Koreans serving in the Communist forces who they said were trained by Soviet advisors. They also said that there was a full Mongolian Cavalry Division from the Mongolian People's Republic serving in China. Regardless of how many Koreans there were, many returned to Korea to form the Korean People's Army in the newly independent North Korea. (US National Archives)

Above: A group photograph of Nationalist junior officers shows them all wearing the army winter coat and fur hat. The fur hats appear to have come in two types, one for other ranks and a better quality one for officers. Double-breasted winter coats were produced with or without fur collars and were modelled on the Japanese Second World War type. Nationalist officers like these changed sides on a regular basis as the war turned against them after 1947. (Philip Jowett)

Opposite above: A lone Nationalist sentry armed with a Thompson sub-machine gun stands guard over a line of Communist prisoners. The campaign in Manchuria did not always go the way of the eventual victors, the Communists. These men may well be given the opportunity of joining the Nationalist Army. Loyal Communists among them would agree with a view to deserting at the earliest opportunity. Some of the best units in the Nationalist Army served in Manchuria and they did not give up the fight easily. (US National Archives)

Opposite below: Nationalist troops move through the mud in a recently captured Manchurian village in 1947. The soldiers are wearing the typical uniform of the Nationalist Army after 1946 with US-type field cap and padded light khaki winter jacket and trousers. They carry their belongings with them as motor transport was not usually available for Chinese troops during the Civil War. (Philip Jowett)

Above: A mortar crew of the Nationalist Army fires their 81mm medium mortar towards Communist positions in the winter of 1947–8. They are protecting their temporary headquarters during an operation against Communist guerrillas. The level of fighting in winter was affected by the severe weather in the North-Eastern provinces of China. Mortars had been important in recent Chinese military campaigns as they were used to compensate for the lack of other types of artillery. The crews are dressed in typical post-1946 uniforms which largely replaced the Second World War-issue uniforms as the Civil War progressed. (Philip Jowett)

Opposite above: A Communist machine-gunner fires his ex-Japanese Taisho 11 light machine gun towards Nationalist lines. Although the Type 11 was an old design, the Communists were happy to receive any weaponry and were given many of this gun by the Soviet Army in 1945–6. He has also acquired an war booty Type 32 steel helmet from the Japanese, and this may again have been handed over to his unit from stores taken in Manchuria in August 1945. First the Japanese and then the Nationalists were the unwilling quartermasters for the Communists during the Civil War. (Philip Jowett)

Opposite below: This Nationalist artillery crew of a US-supplied 75mm PACK howitzer fire their cannon towards Communist lines from the yard of a house in November 1947. They are fighting outside the city of Yingpan in Manchuria trying to stop the Communists from encircling their position. All the crew are wearing the typical winter uniform of the Nationalist Army in the second half of the Civil War. This consisted of a padded light khaki or grey jacket and trousers worn with a US-style peaked cap. The cap was the most common type of headgear worn by the Nationalists after 1946 and often had ear flaps added by the soldiers. (Philip Jowett)

A Nationalist Peace Preservation Corps soldier stands outside his unit office guarding it with a Soviet Moisin-Nagant M1891 rifle in Manchuria. With the lack of a military uniform and his captured Russian rifle he could easily be a Communist guerrilla. The original caption states that he is a paramilitary volunteer of the Nationalist government and the majority of these belonged to the Peace Preservation Corps. (US National Archives)

Chapter Five

The Nationalists Lose Manchuria, 1948

The year 1948 proved to be decisive in the Civil War, with the grave situation for the Nationalists in Manchuria coming to a conclusion. The People's Liberation Army had been able by early 1948 to regroup, retrain and re-arm their armies into a powerful force. They had spent the winter training large numbers of troops in their bases in Northern Manchuria. Many of their new recruits were former Nationalist troops who were, of course, treated with suspicion by the People's Liberation Army. Artillery and other heavy weaponry had been collected together from various sources including items captured in the fighting of 1947. On 8 March the People's Liberation Army attacked several of the Nationalist held towns along the railway system in Manchuria. These assaults were made simultaneously to panic and confuse the nervous Nationalists 'holed up' in their isolated garrisons. In April Chiang Kai-shek declared that he was determined to hold on to the three remaining cities of Changchun, Mukden and Chinchow. He was honest enough to admit that he had lost seven armies including the elite and US-trained New 1st and 6th Armies. With his best units already lost, many of his units in Manchuria were made up of demoralised Southerners who hated serving in the cold North.

The Communist Liao-Shan Offensive began on 12 September and involved twelve Communist divisions. The first target was the city of Ihsien, which fell on 1 October. This allowed the People's Liberation Army to move on to the strategic city of Chinchow, and for 8 divisions to besiege the city along with 100 artillery pieces and 15 tanks. The city was defended by 118,000 Nationalist troops but many of these were southerners from Yunnan province. They and their commanders disobeyed their northern commanders which only added to the problems of the defence. Surrounded and starving, the city fell on 12 October with 34,000 being killed and 88,000 taken prisoner. The fall of Chinchow now left the remaining Nationalist held cities of Changchun and Mukden in desperate straits.

A worried Chiang went to Peking to assess the dilemma facing his armies in Manchuria. After a series of discussions he finally decided after much prompting by his US advisors to give up the fight for Manchuria. His main plan was to save as many of his elite troops as possible from the Manchurian quagmire by moving them southwards out of the region. The objective was for the armies to reach the 'sanctuary' of the Great Wall or get to the ports to be taken by ship southwards. There were still several cities held by the Nationalists with strong garrisons which were well armed and had substantial artillery and armoured vehicles.

Changchun was held by a Nationalist garrison under the command of a general who was secretly negotiating with the Communists. With the city under siege the Nationalist Commander-in-Chief in Manchuria, Wei Li-huang, ordered a large force to go to its relief. The Changchun garrison commander defected to the Communists on 19 October and the city fell to the People's Liberation Army. There was now only the city of Mukden and a few isolated towns in the hands of the Nationalists. With little fight left in any of the Nationalist formations it was only a matter of mopping up the last few strongholds in Manchuria. A final Nationalist counter-offensive launched on 21 October was a last-ditch effort to drive back the People's Liberation Army. This lasted for a week but when it ran out of steam the fate of the Nationalists in Manchuria was finally sealed. Mukden fell on 1 November without much of a fight by the garrison and with some escaping to the port of Yingkow. The only major Nationalist formation was now at the port of Hulutao where the garrison had grown to 137,000 men. These were mostly troops who had retreated from other garrisons and they were glad to be evacuated by the Nationalist Navy. It only remained for the final remnants of the Nationalist Army to escape from the port of Yingkow by sea, with 20,000 managing to do his. The war was now virtually over for the Nationalists who had lost too many troops and too much war materiel in Manchuria. Nationalist losses in Manchuria were 300,000 troops with hundreds of artillery pieces and 75 tanks lost. Chiang Kai-shek had wasted the best of his army in trying to hold on to the whole of China and thereby losing it all.

Opposite above: Proud Communist soldiers of the People's Liberation Army stand on top of a line of Nationalist tanks captured in a recent battle. All the tanks are ex-Japanese models which were handed over to the Nationalists in 1945 and incorporated into their armoured units. The tanks include two Type 97 medium tanks, some armed with 37mm and some with 47mm guns. Many of these tanks were to be driven by Japanese who were forced or at least coerced into serving the Communists. The 90 or so tanks in the People's Liberation Army armoury at this stage in the war were crewed by some of the reported 30,000 Japanese in their ranks. (Cody Images)

Opposite below: A unit of the People's Liberation Army is ready to move forward from their trench during an attack on a Nationalist held town in Manchuria. Although the photograph is not particularly clear, it can be seen that the soldiers are using captured Thompson sub-machine guns and stick grenades. The troops have straw sun hats on their backs which gave protection from the rain in winter and the sun in the summer. (Philip Jowett)

A large formation of Communist troops prepares to go into action against the Nationalists during the summer of 1948. By this time many People's Liberation Army units were well armed, equipped and uniformed largely at the expense of their Nationalist enemies' captured stores. All the troops in this formation appear to have been issued with Japanese M32 steel helmets Among the weapons carried by the heavy weapons squad in the foreground are the Japanese 'knee mortar', used in large numbers by the People's Liberation Army between 1946 and 1949. (Philip Jowett)

This People's Liberation Army soldier fighting in Manchuria in the decisive campaign of 1948 looks like a confident veteran with many years of conflict experience. Although there was a hardcore of men like this in the People's Liberation Army, the majority were either Nationalist 'turncoats' or newly recruited volunteers. On this soldier's cap he wears some kind of commemorative badge of the type issued after major Communist victories. Most Communist troops wore a simple cloth or metal red star on their caps, also often added to captured Nationalist uniforms. (Philip Jowett)

The political officers of a People's Liberation Army unit are pictured during the Manchurian Campaign in 1948 as the war turned to their advantage. As in the Soviet Army, the role of the political officer in a People's Liberation Army unit was vital. Their job was to try and keep the soldiers' morale in their unit high and to deal with any signs of insubordination from its troops. Females like this young officer in the People's Liberation Army had been forced by tradition to break from their family's control in order to volunteer to fight for the revolution. (Philip Jowett)

The reality of the fighting in Manchuria for most of the civilian population is seen here with this despairing elderly refugee from a Nationalist held city. In most of the Nationalist held strongholds of Manchuria the besieged garrisons had to be supplied by air lift in 1947–8. Shortages of food in the cities meant that after the defenders had been fed there was little left for civilians like this starving man. (Philip Jowett)

Above: Another former Japanese Imperial Army vehicle, the Type 91, is seen in the sidings of a Manchurian train station in the summer of 1948. It could be run on roads and rails after a simple adaptation and usually ran ahead of trains to check for damage to the track. With a well-armed crew and an infantry contingent aboard it would be sent out on patrol to try and stop sabotage by Communist supporters and guerrillas. (Philip Jowett)

Opposite above: A Nationalist armoured train moves out of a station in Manchuria to travel to one of the other garrisons still in their hands. The train has an armoured car with firing points down its side for Maxim M1908 heavy machine guns. It also has at least one rotating turret located between the wagons which are also armed with a heavy machine gun. Trains like this were vulnerable to attack by guerrillas and if tracks were torn up they could be isolated and destroyed. In July 1947 the Nationalists controlled 6,250 miles of railway having lost 1,000 miles worth in the previous 3 months. This deterioration was to continue into 1948 as attacks on the lines by Communist guerrillas increased. (Philip Jowett)

Opposite below: The Nationalist crew of an ex-Japanese Type 95 'Soki' armoured vehicle adapted to travel on rails prepare to go out on patrol in Manchuria in 1948. This vehicle was a light tank with retractable wheels which allowed it to be run on rails after a simple 1-minute conversion. Large numbers of armoured railway vehicles and armoured trains were inherited from the Japanese Imperial Army in 1945. Just like the Japanese, the Nationalists used the railway system in Manchuria to keep lines of communication going during the 1946–8 period. (Philip Jowett)

Above: A Communist casualty lies in an abandoned trench on the outskirts of the Manchurian city of Szepingkai. The People's Liberation Army often suffered heavy losses when attacking well-dug-in Nationalist defences. As the Manchurian Campaign wore on the People's Liberation Army chose to encircle Manchurian held towns and cities rather than take them by costly assaults. (Philip Jowett)

Opposite: Lin Piao, the commander of the Communist armies in Manchuria, poses outside his headquarters during the 1948 campaign. He was a Mao loyalist who had served his leader well over the years and had been given his trust in return. Before 1947 Lin led a numerically large but poorly armed and trained force which a year later had been turned into a well-trained and increasingly well-armed force. Much of the credit for the transformation must go to Lin and his officers who by their efforts in Manchuria laid the foundation for Communist victory. (Philip Jowett)

Above: A People's Liberation Army officer gives his troops a morale-boosting talk as they eat their meal after a battle in Manchuria in 1948. The men seem relatively happy as they shiver in their padded cotton winter uniforms while eating their noodles. Although the soldiers of the People's Liberation Army had better morale than their Nationalist foes, the army often suffered high levels of desertion. Not all the troops were volunteers and the Communists often had to resort to press-ganging recruits like the Nationalist Army. (Philip Jowett)

Opposite above: People's Liberation Army soldiers fire towards Nationalist lines with their Japanese Arisaka 98 rifles, Thompson sub-machine guns and light machine guns in the summer of 1948. They are fighting on the outskirts of a Manchurian town held by the Nationalists. All the troops are wearing the light khaki cotton uniforms favoured by both armies in the Civil War. As with weaponry, the People's Liberation Army also acquired huge stores of uniforms and equipment when they captured Nationalist garrisons. (Cody Images)

Opposite below: A US transport plane of the China National Aviation Corporation unloads its cargo of food at a Nationalist garrison in Manchuria. The China National Aviation Corporation and the Civil Air Transport group used a number of US transport planes. These included C46 Commandos, C47 Dakotas and C54 Skymasters to fly in arms and other goods throughout Nationalist held China. Often these planes were the only means of keeping isolated Nationalist garrisons supplied. (Philip Jowett)

People's Liberation Army troops assault the old walled Manchurian city of Chinchow in early October 1948. The city was garrisoned by 150,000 troops with 20,000 being killed during its siege which lasted from 7–15 October. During the siege the defenders were supplied by sea and reinforcements were also landed from Nationalist ships. The reinforcements sent to the city only added to the 80,000 Nationalist prisoners taken when Chinchow fell. Communist forces attacking the city totalled 300,000 with 200 artillery pieces which bombarded the defences relentlessly. When the neighbouring Nationalist held city of Ihsien fell in the first days of October, Chinchow was isolated and its fate was sealed. (Philip Jowett)

Chapter Six

Nationalist Decline, January-October 1948

In January 1948 both sides in the Civil War had huge armies facing each other throughout Northern and Central China. Nationalist forces in Manchuria were claimed to total 400,000 while the People's Liberation Army had 320,000 men. Forces in Northern China were made up of 280,000 Nationalists and 120,000 Communists as Mao gave priority to winning the final victory in Manchuria. He knew that if the struggling Nationalists could be defeated there then huge forces could then advance southwards into Northern China. The compiler of the statistics divided Central China into two theatres, the Yellow River Valley and the Yangtze Valley. There was a hundred-thousand-strong advantage for the Nationalists in the Yellow River theatre with 280,000 of their troops opposed to 180,000. People's Liberation Army troops. Although the Nationalist advantage in the Yangtze Valley was 140,000 against 80,000 Communists, this theatre was to gain more significance over the coming months.

While the fighting was still going on in Manchuria the fighting in North Central Chinese provinces like Shantung, Kiangsu and Hopeh provinces was going the Communist way. In the spring of 1948 the People's Liberation Army took most of the east of the important province of Shantung with fighting ending in April. When fighting resumed in Shantung during July the three months of campaigning ended with the Communist control of most of the province. As in Manchuria, in Shantung province the Nationalists were confined to a few strongholds like the city of Tsingtao. Fighting in Honan province resulted in a victory for the Communists with the taking of the city of Loyang on 17 March after a ten-day siege. Elsewhere in Honan its provincial capital Kaifeng fell to a People's Liberation Army force on 22 May. The city's defence was left to a poorly trained garrison of second-line Peace Preservation Corps troops. In April the propaganda victory of the year before was reversed when Yenan was recaptured by the Communists. To Mao and the Communist leadership the 'liberation' of his old base was of no great importance as the war was going well everywhere else in China.

In July 1948 the relative strengths of the two sides had changed significantly as the People's Liberation Army grew at the expense of the Nationalist Army. The Nationalist strength had fallen by a third compared with their numbers at the start of the Civil War. Nationalist numbers were now at 2,180,000 with just under a million of them armed while the rest were in support units. They still had a large number of artillery pieces with a total of 21,000 and a fair number of tanks and armoured vehicles. They were faced by 1,560,000 People's Liberation Army regulars supported by 700,000 guerrillas and over 22,000 artillery pieces of all types.

Nationalist officials and military officers inspect the dead bodies of a Communist raiding party which had attacked their town near Shanghai in February 1948. The 'bandits', as they were described by the Nationalists, had made a raid on the fortified town and had been defeated by its defenders. All of their bodies had been roped together and put on public display like trophies from a hunt. Their leader's head has been chopped off as a warning to other Communists and is hanging from the wall as a gruesome trophy. (Philip Jowett)

A Nationalist Navy gunboat patrols along the Chinese coast in the summer of 1948 in support of the army. The navy was one part of the Nationalist Armed Forces which managed to maintain its supremacy until the end of the Civil War. Unfortunately for the Nationalists, the Civil War was fought mainly away from the coast and their navy's superiority was not a major factor. The Communists did not import weaponry from abroad so it was not as vital to control China's ports as it was for the Nationalists. (Philip Jowett)

Above: Nationalist militiamen train on parade ground in Shantung province armed only with bamboo spears in April 1948. The militia have been raised by their local military commander to try and reinforce his regular forces. Although many Nationalist commanders had enough rifles to arm all their troops, others were short of all kinds of weaponry. Just like in the 1930s, the amount of weaponry a commander received often depended on his perceived level of loyalty to Chiang Kai-shek. (US National Archives)

Opposite above: People's Liberation Army troops gather around their comrade in a trench who has received a rare letter from home. There was little chance for R & R in either army during the Civil War and any distraction was welcome. Single soldiers would have entertained themselves in the time-honoured way, while married men had other worries. It had been traditional for the families of married soldiers to be with their husbands in garrisons. With little or no chance to send money back to their dependents the Nationalist soldiers still sometimes took their wives and children with them on campaign. (Philip Jowett)

Opposite below: Female militia volunteers in Shantung province in 1948 march past their commander during a parade. The arming of women in the Nationalist Army and its paramilitaries was frowned upon and these girls would probably act as first-aiders. The girls, along with their male comrades, wear black uniforms peculiar to this particular militia force. (US National Archives)

Above: Communist troops inspect recently captured Nationalist artillery which will soon be pressed into service with the People's Liberation Army. The gun in the foreground is an ex-Japanese Type 94 75mm PACK howitzer, which had been introduced in 1934. It was a useful addition to their armoury especially as it broke down into eleven pieces in 30 minutes. In the background is an older Krupp mountain gun which had served with the Chinese Army since the early 1900s. It was surprising that guns like this were captured intact with their breechblocks in place and were seldom spiked. According to reports, the Chinese character meant that soldiers were loath to destroy precious military hardware. This was even the case when they knew that the artillery or other weaponry they did not destroy would fall into enemy hands! (Philip Jowett)

Opposite: Communist troops sort through a large cache of captured Nationalist arms after a battle in 1948. The increasing amount of arms being taken from the Nationalists as the war progressed swung the balance in the People's Liberation Army's favour. Many small arms were ex-Japanese types and some of these had been issued by 1948 to the Nationalist Peace Preservation Corps and village guards. Among the arms seen here are Japanese Type 11 light machine guns, Type 92 medium and Czech ZB-26 light machine guns. (Philip Jowett)

In a rare action photograph a unit of the People's Liberation Army take a position held by Nationalist troops. These Nationalist troops readily surrender to their Communist counterparts who will take the enemy weapons and hand them to their comrades. Rank and file Nationalist troops were usually given the opportunity to join the People's Liberation Army's ranks and many took up the offer. Many Nationalist troops had been pressed into service and some would have preferred to go home to their villages rather than fight for the Communists. (Philip Jowett)

A young Communist grenadier carries a large number of German type stick grenades in pouches and attached by string to his back. When there were insufficient small arms to go around younger soldiers like this boy would be given any available weapons. These roughly made grenades had been produced in Chinese arsenals and workshops in China since the early 1930s. (Philip Jowett)

A barefoot boy stands forlornly in the rubble of his house which has been damaged in fighting between the Communists and Nationalists. He clutches a book he has retrieved from the remains of his family home and looks for reassurance. By February 1948 there were a total of 29 million displaced people throughout war-torn China, with 3 million in Manchuria alone. In Northern China there were 6 million refugees, and 10 million each in Central and Southern China. As in all previous civil conflicts in China in the twentieth century, the ordinary people suffered most during the 1946–9 fighting. Many just wanted the war to end and did not really care who won as long as their victory brought peace. (Philip Jowett)

Chapter Seven

THE HUAI-HAI CAMPAIGN, NOVEMBER 1948– JANUARY 1949

After the defeat of the Nationalist Army in Manchuria and the advance of the People's Liberation Army across the Great Wall into Northern China heavy fighting continued into late 1948. The next major campaign was to be fought in North-Central China in the large flat region north of the Yangtze River. This campaign was named after the proximity of the Huai River and the Lunghai Railway giving it the title of the Huai-hai Campaign. Fought over a 200km front and involving almost 2,000,000 troops, this campaign was to be the largest battle since the Second World War. Originally Chiang Kai-shek had planned to fight the campaign just north of the Yangtze River but it was decided to move the Nationalist defence line 100 miles further north. This new front line encompassed the junctions of the most important railways in Northern China above the Yangtze. Chiang knew that if this strategic region fell to the Communists then the fate of Nationalist China was virtually sealed.

Chiang chose the city of Hsuchow to be the place where his Nationalist Army would make its decisive stand. Hsuchow was turned into a bastion of the Nationalist front and was reinforced with 150,000 troops as the 500,000 troops of the People's Liberation Army approached. Facing the Communist offensive were a similar number of Nationalist troops with 200,000 of the 500,000 organised into the 7th Army Group. The 7th was under the command of General Huang Po-tao and was positioned to the west of the strategic city of Hsuchow. The remainder were in the 2nd Army Group under General Chiu Ching-chuan and they were to the east of Hsuchow. With a total of 300,000 troops, the city was expected to be able to resist the People's Liberation Army attacks and initially they did. Communist advances towards Hsuchow were halted in mid-November but these soon resumed as the People's Liberation Army tried to outflank the city's defences. By the end of the month the city was more or less surrounded by the highly mobile People's Liberation Army troops of the 2nd and 3rd Field Armies. People's Liberation Army advances also took them to the Nationalist held town of Suhsien, 40 miles to the south of the city. Suhsien was completely surrounded and its 140,000-strong garrison was unable to go to the aid of the beleaguered forces there.

As conditions in Hsuchow deteriorated it was decided that the garrison should break out to the south-west. At the same time the Nationalist 12th Army Group was to advance north-eastwards to link up with the withdrawing troops. At the beginning of December 1948 the break-out by 230,000 soldiers and 100,000 civilians began. Communist troops were waiting in ambush for the retreating Nationalist horde and immediately began to make attacks on the disorganised force. By mid-December the slow-moving Nationalists were surrounded in the open plains and were losing thousands of troops through desertion each day. The Nationalist Army was still too large to defeat in a large set-piece battle and anyway less costly 'hit and run' attacks on the demoralised troops were doing the trick. The 12th Army Group was isolated and surrounded and had to surrender on 15 December. This ended any hope that the combined 16th, 2nd and 13th Army Group had of being rescued and their fate was sealed. To his credit the Nationalist commander, General Tu Yu-ming, refused Chiang's offer of a mission to rescue him and his staff. Tu was honourable enough to not want to desert his army as defeat became inevitable. Other commanders including Chiang Kai-shek's son did escape from the trap their forces were in.

Chiang Kai-shek did not want huge amounts of men and equipment to fall into Communist hands. In a meeting in Nanking he agreed that the aerial bombardment of his own troops was an option. Word of this decision reached his commanders trapped by the People's Liberation Army and this helped to persuade them that the time had come to give up the fight. On 10 January 1949 the surrounded Nationalists finally surrendered with over 320,000 troops having been captured during the campaign. The People's Liberation Army now moved southwards towards the north bank of the Yangtze River and the final barrier to the taking of Central and Southern China.

Above: A 105mm M101 howitzer of the Nationalist Army fires towards Communist lines from its dug-in position in the besieged city of Hsuchow. This modern field gun was sold to the Nationalists in large numbers but never in sufficient quantities to replace older models. The city was to come under increasing pressure and it was decided to try and save some of the garrison by attempting a break-out. On 1 December 1948 before dawn 230,000 troops and 100,000 civilians left the burning city. Within 2 weeks 200,000 starving troops and their dependents had been surrounded by the pursuing People's Liberation Army and were taken into captivity. (Philip Jowett)

Opposite above: People's Liberation Army soldiers sort out captured small arms and machine guns taken in a battle with the Nationalist Army. The booty taken by the Communist troops includes a number of Maxim M1908 heavy machine guns. These and the other weapons would be quickly sorted and distributed to volunteers who had been acting as porters or other support troops for the People's Liberation Army. Fortunately for the Communists, the Nationalists often served as 'involuntary' quartermasters for them. (Philip Jowett)

Opposite below: This Nationalist trench on the outskirts of the city of Hsuchow is a typical dug-in position on the open plains of Central China during the campaign. Chiang Kai-shek had decided to move his defence line for the vital campaign north from the Huai-Hai River to Hsuchow. It was the fighting for entrenched positions like this that was to decide the future of the campaign and the future of China. (Philip Jowett)

The two-man crew of a Hotchkiss M1914 medium machine gun fires from a dugout during the fighting for Hsuchow in 1948. Their position has been camouflaged by using matting to break up the outline of the emplacement. Hotchkiss machine guns could easily be served by a smaller crew as it only required one man to fire and the other to feed in the strips of ammunition from the left side. Both crewmen have straw mantles over their shoulders to protect their uniforms when carrying the two parts of the gun when dismantled. (Philip Jowett)

These Communist machine-gunners are well kitted out with uniforms and equipment and are prepared with their large shovels to dig-in to new positions during the Huaihai Campaign. All three soldiers have ex-Japanese steel helmets either captured from the Japanese or Nationalist Armies. Their back packs are really well organised bundles with one man having a spare pair of shoes strapped to his. They are firing a captured Type 24 heavy machine gun captured from the Nationalist Army in an earlier engagement. (Philip Jowett)

Two Nationalist machine-gunners in the Huai-hai Campaign sit on the edge of their dugout armed with their Bren light machine gun. The Bren gun was supplied by the UK in small numbers but the majority in use with the Nationalists came from Canada. During the 1948 fighting the Nationalist Army spent much of their time holding defensive positions against the increasingly mobile People's Liberation Army. The morale of Nationalist troops like these was not helped by the lack of any offensive action by their commanders. (Philip Jowett)

Nationalist infantry fire their small arms from their hill-top position during the Huai-hai Campaign in late 1948. The rifleman is armed with a Mauser 98k, or its Chinese-made copy the 'Chiang Kai-shek' rifle. Despite the supply of large amounts of modern US small arms, the Mauser was to continue in Nationalist service up to and beyond the end of the Civil War. The rifleman's comrade is armed with a Thompson M1A1 sub-machine gun supplied by the USA during the Second World War. (Philip Jowett)

A People's Liberation Army light machine-gun crew fire their ZB-26 light machine gun towards Nationalist positions during the Huai-hai Campaign. All the machine-gun crew and accompanying infantry have camouflaged their field caps with grass pushed into their hat bands. These troops are taking part in one of the thousands of small actions which made up the two-month Huai-hai campaign. (Philip Jowett)

Chiang Wei-kuo, the adopted son of Chiang Kai-shek, arrives at the front during the Huai-hai Campaign in a liaison plane smiling for the news cameras. Chiang Wei-kuo had spent a number of years in Nazi Germany as an officer trainee in the 1930s and served in a German armoured unit in 1938. He was put in charge of an armoured unit equipped with M5 light tanks during the Huai-hai campaign. According to reports, his unit performed well during the campaign with Chiang utilising all the training he had received in Germany. (Philip Jowett)

A line of Nationalist M5 light tanks under the command of Chiang Wei-kuo are ready to go into action against the People's Liberation Army. Although the USA supplied a number of these tanks to the Nationalists, it was never in sufficient numbers to counter the rise of the Communists. During the Burma Campaign in 1944–5 the Chinese tankers had been loath to risk their 'precious' tanks in action. It was not through lack of courage that the Nationalist tanks were sometimes held back in battle but just through fear of losing irreplaceable weaponry. During the battle for Hsuchow the People's Liberation Army suffered a reverse when a unit of these M5 light tanks launched a surprise attack. This assault was led by Chiang and was one of the few successes in a series of setbacks for the Nationalists. This attack was backed up for once by strong air support and some of the best troops in the People's Liberation Army were defeated. As one correspondent said, for once the Nationalist Army had 'held its own against some of the best PLA troops'. (Philip Jowett)

Above: A column of Communist soldiers file past a few mountain and light artillery pieces recently captured from the Nationalist Army. The variety of weaponry in service with the Nationalists and then by proxy with the Communists made the logistics for both armies difficult. These guns would be assessed by the Communist artillerymen, many of who were former Nationalist troops to see which could be put back into service. As the Communists captured better quality weaponry the older and less serviceable guns would be abandoned by them. (Philip Jowett)

Opposite above: Although a number of these M5 light tanks were supplied by the USA to the Nationalists, there were not enough of them to overwhelm the People's Liberation Army. Most Nationalist tankers had begun their careers in the Provisional Tank Group which fought alongside the Allies in Burma in 1944–5. When they were transferred back to China in 1945 they were not allowed to take their medium Sherman M4 tanks with them. These light M5 tanks proved to be effective during the Civil War fighting against the ex-Japanese tanks which formed the People's Liberation Army's armoured force. (Philip Jowett)

Opposite below: Communist troops pose in front of a haul of recently captured machine guns including many ZB-26 light machine guns. This weapon was the most common model in service with the Chinese Army during the 1930s and 1940s. The heavier weapons are French Hotchkiss M1914s used by the Nationalist Army along with other types. There are also a couple of Taisho 11 Japanese light machine guns among the pile of war booty weapons. (Philip Jowett)

Above: A column of Communist troops move up to the front line during the encirclement of the Nationalist positions around Hsuchow. The soldiers carry their equipment in improvised backpacks that were really bundles attached to a bamboo frame. Neither side in the Civil War had much time for military smartness and the men are wearing the usual cotton uniforms. These were made of thin cotton in summer and wadded or padded cotton in the winter with the field cap worn by both armies. (Philip Jowett)

Opposite above: This US M101 105mm howitzer is being fired from an artillery position in the interior of the defences of Hsuchow. The crew fires the gun towards People's Liberation Army lines while the loaders take shelter a few yards away which suggests that enemy artillery is firing back. The Nationalist Army had a defensive doctrine that would result in victory for their more aggressive People's Liberation Army foes. It had always been said that the Chinese soldier had always been stubbornly brave in defence throughout the centuries. (Philip Jowett)

Opposite below: While the fate of the Nationalist held city of Hsuchow in Northern Kiangsu was still in doubt this machine-gunner and his comrade service their Maxim heavy machine gun. They are cleaning and oiling the gun after firing off 3,000 rounds the night before as they helped capture a village. When asked how many Communists he had killed during the firefight he said, 'I can't count the Communists in the dark but it must be countless.' (Philip Jowett)

Above: During the fighting for Hsuchow during the Huai-hai Campaign in December 1948 a group of Nationalist grenadiers wait to go forward to attack Communist trenches. Their comrades are preparing to fire a light mortar towards enemy positions to soften them up before their attack is launched. Hsuchow was in the direct line of the advance of the People's Liberation Army towards the Nationalist capital at Nanking. During November fighting took place in the villages and towns on the outskirts of Hsuchow before it fell to the Communists on 3 December. (Philip Jowett)

Opposite above: A Nationalist signalman communicates with his forward observation posts to check on the movements of the Communists around the city of Hsuchow. From his thatched camouflaged dugout he will try and find any Communist targets for Nationalist artillery to shell. His efforts would all be in vain as the city fell to the Communists a few days later and this man and his comrades would be in retreat. (Philip Jowett)

Opposite below: People's Liberation Army soldiers joyfully celebrate their victory in the Huai-hai Campaign and the fall of Hsuchow. Within a few months these confident troops will be taking part in the crossing of the Yangtze River and the final stages of the Civil War. Even though final victory is a year away, the People's Liberation Army will spend the rest of the war notching up victory after victory over the Nationalists. (Philip Jowett)

Chapter Eight

Nationalists in Despair, December 1948–April 1949

The defeat of the Nationalists during the Huai-hai campaign and the fall of their bulwark in the city of Hsuchow caused widespread panic in Nanking, 200 miles to the south. Although there were large numbers of Nationalist troops to the region to the South of Hsuchow, they were largely demoralised. The Nationalists now moved south-eastwards towards Nanking, fighting a series of poorly organised rear-guard actions. The People's Liberation Army captured the cities of Sushsien and Pengpu, 85 miles from the capital, and the Nationalists were pushed along like sheep being herded to their fate. A large number of Nationalist troops ended up at the railway junction at Pukow on the north bank of the Yangtze opposite Nanking. They were not allowed to cross the river into temporary safety in Nanking and many fell into Communist hands. With little leadership from their commanders, thousands of these Nationalist troops who could have fought in the defence of Nanking were wasted.

By April 1949 the People's Liberation Army's 2nd Field Army under Liu Po-cheng and the 3rd Field Army under Ch'en Yi were ready to cross the Yangtze. They crossed the river on 20 April mainly by junks and other small boats but did not come under fire from the Nationalists on the south bank. Chiang Kai-shek had resigned his post as President and his successor Li Tsung-jen was looking for a way to negotiate peace. He had hoped to stop the People's Liberation Army from crossing the Yangtze to give him a stronger hand in any peace deal. If he could maintain control of China south of the Yangtze, he might be able to negotiate peace with Mao Tse-tung. Unfortunately for the Nationalists and Li, his Army was too weak and divided to put up any kind of a fight and the People's Liberation Army crossed the Yangtze. Immediately they moved towards the Nationalist capital at Nanking where officials had already decamped to the new capital at Canton.

A friendly peasant points out the lie of the land around the Nationalist positions to a People's Liberation Army officer. The Chinese people were generally more disposed to the Communists as many were tired of Nationalist rule. Any support for the Nationalists outside the main cities and towns was ruthlessly suppressed by the Communists. Even if peasants had loyalty to Chiang Kai-shek, they were often wise to keep this to themselves. This was especially the case at the war turned more and more against the Nationalists from mid-1948 onwards. (Philip Jowett)

Nationalist soldiers withdraw from Pengpu, north of Nanking as the Communists move towards the city. These troops are carrying all their kit and personal effects slung from poles over their shoulders in the old Chinese manner. According to the photograph's caption, these troops are being reorganised to try and launch a counter-offensive against the People's Liberation Army. The man in the foreground has a US-supplied Springfield rifle slung over his shoulder. (Philip Jowett)

Above: This People's Liberation Army machine-gun team pose proudly for the Communist propaganda cameraman during a battle. By the time this photograph was taken the People's Liberation Army was preparing to move across the Yangtze River and was mopping up the last remnants of Nationalist resistance. The soldiers show off a variety of weaponry with a Japanese Arisaka rifle and Type 3 medium machine gun. One man has a C-96 semi-automatic pistol while the other holds a Czech ZB-26 light machine gun. (Philip Jowett)

Opposite above: Nationalist troops file past a casualty station as they move out of Pukow during the December 1948 fighting. The indifference of their fit comrades for the wounded was largely due to the harsh reality of life in the Nationalist Army. Any enemy wounded could expect even less care if that were possible and there were many cases of captured injured being shot. One Western correspondent noted that many of the Communist dead had battle wounds but appeared to have been 'finished off' with a single bullet to the back of their heads. (Philip Jowett)

Opposite below: In early December 1948 troops leave Pukow railway station as they move out to reinforce their forces trying to stop the Communists from severing the railway line south of Pengpu. Pukow is just to the north of the Nationalist capital Nanking and was a concentration point for Nationalist troops battling the Communists. (Philip Jowett)

Above: Nationalist stretcher bearers bring in the wounded from the fighting around Pukow in December 1948 to a treatment station. The Nationalist wounded received little in the way of medical care when they eventually got to the aid station. With so few army doctors the best they could hope for would be an often dirty bandage to dress the wound. This lack of care meant that few wounded were ever fit enough to return to the front line and the resultant wastage crippled the Nationalist Army. (Philip Jowett)

Opposite above: Nationalist troops in Pukow railway station take a meal break while waiting for goods trains to take them towards the battle. They could also be taken away from the fighting depending on the outcome of the battle for the city. As 1948 drew to a close there were still large formations of Nationalist troops in the field in Central China. Many of these armies, divisions and smaller units would increasingly be taken over en mass into service with the People's Liberation Army by their commanders. (Philip Jowett)

Opposite below: Nationalist soldiers in their open goods trucks wait patiently to be transported away from Pukow railway station. In the confused situation that existed around Pukow these soldiers would just be grateful to get on any train leaving the city. Many of these troops were moved through the railway system to new concentration areas further south. These troops had largely been refused permission to cross the Yangtze River to enter the capital at Nanking. News reports in early December reported that military and civilian refugees were arriving in safer cities like Canton and Chungking. (Philip Jowett)

Above: A mortar crew of the People's Liberation Army moves up towards Nationalist positions with their US 81mm mortar. Throughout the 1920s and 1930s the Chinese Army had made widespread use of mortars often as a substitute for heavier artillery. Both the Communists and Nationalists used several types of mortar during the Civil War with the US 60mm light and 81mm medium being the most common. Of course, any Japanese mortars taken in 1945 were used as long as the ammunition stocks held out. (Cody Images)

Opposite above: A division of Nationalist cavalry rides through the outskirts of Nanking in December 1948. These troopers are part of an elite formation which was loyal to Chiang unlike many of their comrades by this stage of the war. They are well armed with modern M2 carbines which were supplied in large numbers by the USA during the Civil War. Although most of the men are well mounted, one trooper appears to have been given a smaller and less robust specimen of horseflesh to ride. (Philip Jowett)

Opposite below: In preparation for the expected Communist attack on the Nationalist capital at Nanking civilians dig defensive ditches. Throughout the winter of 1948–9 Nanking expected to be attacked but before this could happen the People's Liberation Army would have to cross the Yangtze River. The river was just to the north of the city and its citizens knew that once the enemy crossed it Nanking would fall within a few days. (Philip Jowett)

勝利渡長江

Above: This Communist propaganda poster shows the landing of the 2nd and 3rd People's Liberation Army Armies on the south bank of the Yangtze. This romanticised version of the crossing of the Yangtze shows the courageous People's Liberation Army units landing on the bank and cutting through the defences. In reality the defence of the Yangtze by the Nationalists was poorly organised and their forces were overstretched. The crossing of the river was mainly by junk, although some swam across clinging to straw rafts or inflated pigskins. (Philip Jowett)

Opposite: Even as the resistance of the Nationalist Army was coming to an end the government was trying to bring in new weaponry. These US Army surplus M5 light tanks are being loaded onto a ship in Houston, Texas to be shipped to the Nationalist Army in Shanghai in mid-November 1948. The M5 was obsolete in the US Army but was capable of fulfilling a useful role in the Civil War and was used in some numbers. Many Nationalist tanks ended up in service with the People's Liberation Army, often crewed by drivers and other crew who had been captured by the Communists. Others were transported to the Nationalist bastion on the island of Formosa in preparation for the evacuation of the mainland. (Philip Jowett)

In this rather poor photograph People's Liberation Army assault troops charge ashore on the south bank of the Yangtze on 22 April. These troops are under heavy fire from the Nationalist defenders while in other sectors they crossed unopposed. In some parts of the battlefield the Communists laid down a heavy bombardment before they crossed the river. Other crossing points saw People's Liberation Army commandos crossing the Yangtze in complete silence and with no defenders waiting for them. (Philip Jowett)

These larger junks transport whole units of People's Liberation Army troops across the Yangtze, which at its widest point was 3km across. The defence of the south bank of the river was not helped by the fact that some Nationalist commanders refused to obey the orders of their superiors. In addition, the mutiny of part of the Nationalist River Fleet upriver from the crossing points helped the People's Liberation Army to cross more easily. (Philip Jowett)

Chapter Nine

Fall Of The North - Nationalist Defeat in Northern China, 1948-9

After the defeat of the Nationalists during the Huai-hai Campaign their forces in Northern China were largely cut off by the advancing People's Liberation Army. The Communists could now easily leave the Nationalists in the North to 'wither on the vine' and Peking was not a strategic target. To Mao and his leadership Peking and the other northern cities were only of importance because of their prestige. Mao had already decided that Peking would once again become the nation's capital replacing the 'hated' Nationalist capital at Nanking. The Nationalist Army in the North had been largely ignored by the leadership in Nanking and had been starved of funds and military supplies. In 1948 the funding sent by the USA to support the armed forces of Nationalist China was $125,000,000. Out of this total $87 million went to the Nationalist ground forces, the Nationalist Air Force $29 million and the Nationalist Navy $9.5 million. The money for the ground forces was not, however, distributed evenly and the Nationalists in Northern China were starved of resources.

The main Nationalist commander in Northern China, General Fu Tso-yi, was in a dilemma as to what to do with his 375,000 troops. Out of this total Fu counted nearly a quarter of a million of these troops as being personally loyal to him. This gave him an advantage in any future negotiations with the Communists if he chose to surrender. In the meantime, Fu had to decide how best to defend Northern China against the Communists. He could either concentrate them in the Peking-Tientsin region or send some of them to help other beleaguered Nationalist generals in the North. Like most Nationalist military leaders in the Civil War Fu decided to look after his own interests and kept his forces close at hand. Fu was a pragmatic man who saw the reality of his precarious position in 1948 and was looking for a way out. He knew that he could not expect much material support from the Nationalist government. By the autumn of 1948 he controlled a small region in Northern China with 40 divisions and 98 aircraft. Although his forces looked formidable, he knew that the 130,000 Communists opposing him would soon receive reinforcements. These would come from the victorious armies that had recently won the Huai-hai Campaign. At the same time he could expect little reinforcements himself from the Nationalists in Central China. He knew that the rapidly expanding People's Liberation Army would soon be in a position to challenge him and probably defeat him. Fu continued to claim he was ready to defend the North to the 'last man' he was prepared to negotiate a peaceful handover of Peking and the region to the Communists. In the meantime his situation was boosted by the expected arrival of $125 million in US aid for his forces. Although this material aid was welcome, Fu had other problems such as the large number of refugees who had fled from the Communists that he was trying to feed.

By January 1949 much of Northern and Eastern China was already in the hands of the Communists with the Nationalists isolated in the two cities of Tientsin and Peking. These two cities and the regions around them were protected by relatively strong Nationalist forces. The sixty-four-day campaign by the People's Liberation Army's 4th Field Army led to fall of all of Northern China, with the last major cities Tientsin and Peking succumbing in January 1949. When Tientsin fell on 15 January the 130,000-strong garrison was lost having been outnumbered by the 340,000 Communists. The battle for the city of Tientsin was fierce with some of Fu's best troops defending it to the last man. When it fell on 15 January it was obvious to Fu that his days were numbered and he began negotiating in earnest with the Communists. General Fu Tso-yi surrendered Peking on 22 January after negotiating a peaceful handover to the People's Liberation Army.

Mao moved to the city immediately and proclaimed the city as the restored capital of China in place of the 'despised' Nationalist capital Nanking. The day before Chiang had made one of his many resignations handing over power to General Li Tsung-jen, his long-term rival.

While the campaign for the capture of Peking was ongoing, the other stronghold of the Nationalists was in Shansi province. Although most of the province was in Communist hands by late 1948 two large Nationalist garrisons held out against their attacks. The Taiyuan Campaign, which lasted from October 1948 until April 1949, was really a siege of the two cities still held by the Nationalists in the province of Shansi. Taiyuan the provincial capital had a garrison of 130,000, while the other Nationalist held city, Tatung, had only 10,000 men defending it. When the two cities fell there were desperate scenes as cut off garrisons including Japanese volunteers fought to the death. The plight of the Northern Nationalist forces was now of little interest to Chiang and his leadership. He had other worries in trying to defend his political heartland in Central and Southern China.

Communist troops move across a river in front of a Nationalist held town in Hopeh province during their campaign against the Nationalists. In 1946 the Communists held about a third of the province, while the Nationalists held slightly less than a third. The other third was being fought over by Nationalist divisions and a large force of Communist guerrillas. By 1948 the Nationalists had been pushed out of Hopeh by Lin Piao's forces moving south from Manchuria. (Cody Images)

People's Liberation Army troops make an assault on the town of Langchow as the fighting for Northern China comes to a conclusion. The Nationalist forces in Northern China received little support from the government in Nanking. General Fu Tso-yi, the Commander-in-Chief of the Nationalist forces in the North, had plenty of troops but did not receive the same amount of war materiel as other generals. After the fall of Manchuria there were large numbers of People's Liberation Army troops like these available to take on Fu's army. (Philip Jowett)

Communist forces begin an attack on the outskirts of the Shansi capital, Taiyuan, which was garrisoned by 150,000 Nationalist troops. The Shansi warlord, Marshal Yen Hsi-shan, had vowed to defend the city to the last man and to take a vial of poison rather than surrender. He instead fled his long-time headquarters in the city and left its defence largely to Japanese mercenaries, many of whom did fight until the last bullet. (Philip Jowett)

A heavily overloaded government train prepares to leave the railway station of a Northern Chinese city in late 1948. The passengers clinging to the front of the engine included several Nationalist soldiers. In the scramble to escape the surrounded city many passengers climbed onto the roof of the carriages. Keeping the railway network open in Northern China and Manchuria was a priority for the Nationalist government. (Philip Jowett)

A well-posed photograph of a People's Liberation Army soldier during a training exercise in Northern China. He is kitted out courtesy of his nation's former tormentors, the Japanese, with an Imperial Army M32 steel helmet and a Type 99 cavalry carbine. It appears that the soldier has been issued with a backpack with an entrenching shovel on his back. The quality of equipment supplied to soldiers on both sides varied from one unit to another with the best units receiving the better kit. This was even the case in the supposedly egalitarian People's Liberation Army. (Philip Jowett)

Soldiers of General Fu Tso-yi's Nationalist 94th Corps prepare to move out on an operation to open up the Peking–Suiyuan Railway. This operation, which began in the autumn of 1948, had the aim of keeping this important line of communication open. Many Nationalist campaigns by this stage of the Civil War were aimed only at maintaining control of ever decreasing enclaves in Northern and Central China. (Philip Jowett)

Above: Nationalist troops set up camp in the grounds of the Temple of Heaven in the Forbidden City of Peking in November 1948. While the troops of General Fu Tso-yi were well trained, when the former capital of China fell it was not following a siege but was after negotiation between the pragmatic Fu and the Communist command. (Philip Jowett)

Opposite above: Cavalry of Fu Tso-yi's Nationalist Cavalry gather before going on an operation in defence of Peking against the Communists. Fu received little support from Chiang in Nanking and tried to buy his own armaments from the UK and Belgium. These included an order for 20,000 machine guns and 100,000 rifles from the UK and 6,000 machine guns, 3,000 sub-machine guns and 100,000 rifles from Belgium. His troopers are armed with Sten sub-machine guns which he has purchased from the UK or Canada. Fu was frustrated with the lack of help he got from his leader and this led to him regarding his command as independent of Chiang. (Philip Jowett)

Opposite below: Two Communist cavalrymen ride along a river bank through a town on the outskirts of Peking wearing typical winter uniforms. The Communists had used large numbers of cavalry during their war against the Japanese in 1937–45. When the Civil War began they expanded their mounted forces whenever they could capture horses from the Nationalists. In the vast expanses covered by the fighting in the Civil War cavalry was important for reconnaissance and scouting missions. (US National Archives)

The cover of the illustrated section of the *New York Times Magazine* from 23 January 1949 shows an old man searching through the rubble of his bombed house. In the distance are the walls of the old capital of China and his family wait for him to finish his work. Fortunately for the people of Peking, the city was taken over by the Communists after negotiations by the city's garrison commander General Fu Tso-yi. (Philip Jowett)

A well-turned out cavalry unit of the People's Liberation Army rides into the centre of Peking. After the surrender of General Fu Tso-yi the peaceful takeover of Peking came as a relief to the city's population. These men belong to the 4th Field Army which captured the old capital and are wearing newly issued uniforms. All the troopers have ex-Japanese steel helmets and Arisaka Type 98 rifles taken from Japanese stores in Soviet hands. During the Civil War there were repeated reports of the Soviet Union supplying their own armaments to the People's Liberation Army. These accounts said that rifles, machine guns and shells for the People's Liberation Army's artillery were coming direct from Russian factories. (Philip Jowett)

Victorious Communist troops enter Peking in January 1949 after the city's garrison had negotiated a peaceful end to the campaign to take it. They are led by an ex-Japanese Type 95 light tank with several of its crew sat on top of it to take the applause of the crowd. Most Chinese people by the time Peking fell in 1949 were weary after several decades of civil conflict. Even pro-Nationalist civilians were often relieved that the war was coming to an end and simply yearned for peace. (Philip Jowett)

Above: This large-scale pro-Communist demonstration is taking place in of the squares of Peking just after the victory of the People's Liberation Army in Northern China. The ordinary people of Northern China were in general happy that the Civil War for them was over and stable government was now in place. Northern China had been neglected by the Nationalist government since it came to power in the late 1920s. The region had suffered eight years of occupation by the Japanese and then several years of civil conflict. (Philip Jowett)

Opposite above: Disciplined and smartly turned out People's Liberation Army soldiers march into the centre of Peking a few days after their first entry into the city. The official takeover of the city was on 31 January and like other cities victory parades continued for a few days. Every victory was exploited to the full by a Communist propaganda ministry which had spent many years honing its skills. The People's Liberation Army's victories during the Civil War were seen from the outside as revolutionary in nature but in reality they were hard-won military victories delivered by a well-trained and, by 1949, well-armed army. (Philip Jowett)

Opposite below: People's Liberation Army officers inspect a collection of captured Nationalist armoured cars in Peking in January 1949. These armoured vehicles were produced in several government workshops and came in four or five different versions. All these models of improvised armoured cars were limited in armament with heavy machine guns being the normal weapons. As with all other Nationalist equipment, the Communists introduced any serviceable captured vehicles into their service. The People's Liberation Army appears to have also produced their own light armoured car in small numbers in their workshops. (Philip Jowett)

Chapter Ten

The Fall of Shanghai, 25 May 1949

After the crossing of the Yangtze River by the People's Liberation Army in mid-April 1949, the important city of Shanghai with its population of 6 million was now under serious threat. Shanghai had been the commercial hub of China since the late 1890s and was where the majority of Chinese money was created and banked. Its importance to Nationalist China in 1937 meant that it had been defended bravely but futilely by Chiang Kai-shek's troops. After a titanic struggle with the invading Japanese Imperial Army, costing several hundred thousand Chinese dead, the city fell. After the defeat of the Japanese in August 1945 the city's previous importance was soon restored and it should have been defended as resolutely as it had been twelve years before.

The reality was that although the Nationalist leadership claimed to be ready to fight for Shanghai to the 'last man', few believed the rhetoric. Shanghai was defended 'on paper' by a substantial Nationalist force of 150,000 troops. Many of these soldiers were survivors of the defence of the Yangtze River and had poor morale. At least 150,000 troops had been lost in trying to stop the People's Liberation Army from crossing the Yangtze so the garrison was not at full strength. Shanghai was not properly fortified and the military leadership in the city had already given up before the fighting began. Chiang Kai-shek had flown into Shanghai to assess the situation and had quickly come to the conclusion that its fate was sealed. He then flew to Formosa to take a holiday and get over the expected loss of the city which was vital to his government's survival. He left behind a city that was flooded with refugees, some of who had recently arrived because Shanghai was the only place where they could withdraw their savings. The military crisis in Shanghai was mirrored in a financial crisis that meant that 1 US dollar was now worth 25 million Chinese dollars by 25 May. Chinese dollars had dropped in value by 50 per cent over the night of 24 May as the city was about to fall.

As the People's Liberation Army advanced on the city the majority of the garrison sat and waited for the inevitable. One Nationalist unit, the 123rd Corps, performed a clever manoeuvre which halted the People's Liberation Army advance at least temporarily. The brave defence of the 123rd took the People's Liberation Army by surprise and largely halted their advance for seventeen days but did not stop the city from falling. This respite was unfortunately not taken advantage of and when the Communists arrived in front of Shanghai it was taken without much fighting. There were pockets of resistance but these were soon dealt with by the first People's Liberation Army troops that entered the city.

A well-armed and determined looking Nationalist sentry stands at his guard post outside Shanghai protected by barbed wire and armed with a Thompson sub-machine gun. The city was defended by 210,000 troops in 25 divisions with 20 given the task of defending the western approaches. The garrison included all uniformed personnel available including five divisions of traffic police. As all Nationalist police were armed as well as the army they were expected to fight to protect the regime when it was under threat. (Philip Jowett)

Above: Two government armoured cars protect a Shanghai bank as crowds gather to try and withdraw their funds. Shanghai was the commercial centre of Nationalist China and a number of international banks had their headquarters there. The ordinary people of Shanghai had more of a financial stake in the Nationalist government than anywhere else in China. Any rumour that might affect the security and value of the people's savings resulted in widespread panic and scenes like this. (Philip Jowett)

Opposite above: In December 1948 citizens of Shanghai scramble to change their practically worthless money at a bank. The lines of desperate people wound around the block and fights broke out as people tried to jump the queue. Ten people were killed in the crush during the 24 hours it took for the situation to calm down. This kind of panic was part of the uncertainty that blighted Nationalist China during the Civil War. Peoples savings were swallowed up by currency crises brought on by the poor management of the economy. (Philip Jowett)

Opposite below: Nationalist troops moving through Shanghai during their withdrawal rest in the streets of the city on 1 February. According to the photograph caption, this unit is being temporarily billeted in buildings which had previously been used by the US Army. The general demeanour of the soldiers shows the lack of morale of the Nationalist Army in early 1949. As 1949 progressed the Nationalist Army's long retreat was to sap the last of the fighting spirit of the majority of its troops. (Philip Jowett)

Above: Nationalist troops move up to the defences of Shanghai on 23 April 1949 carrying US-supplied 57mm recoiless rifles. The commander of the Shanghai garrison, General Tang En-po, vowed to turn the city into another Stalingrad. He had a strong garrison and was confident of being able to defend the city against the encircling 3rd Red Army. His boasts turned out to be hollow, however, as the city was to prove impossible to defend and its garrison were not up for the fight. (Philip Jowett)

Opposite above: A government merchant ship sits at anchor in the harbour at Shanghai waiting to be loaded with civilians to be evacuated further south. As was usual during the Civil War, civilians with money to bribe their way onto ships or even aircraft could get away from Shanghai. It was the middle class and rich who had most to lose by a Communist victory and it was not surprising that they wanted to flee before such an eventuality. As the People's Liberation Army advance continued the rich would find it harder to keep escaping the clutches of the Communists. (Philip Jowett)

Opposite below: In a scene that aptly sums up the situation of the Nationalist Army during the Civil War an officer takes a ride in one of his unit's carts in March 1949. Sitting in the back of the cart, he is transporting fodder back to his unit in Shanghai while one of his soldiers guides the mule. The officer does not exactly imbue confidence in the Nationalist Army's leadership and both men look demoralised. Nationalist officers were often corrupt and exploited the areas they controlled by extracting local taxes from the people often under the noses of honest officials. Chiang Kai-shek asked that the world should not judge his army too harshly regarding corruption as it had always been endemic in the Chinese military! (Philip Jowett)

Above: A Nationalist armoured car patrols the streets of Shanghai in early May 1949 during the build-up to the defence of the city. These armoured cars were built in several government workshops and a number of different models were produced armed with machine guns or light cannons. This car has a number of Maxim Type 24 water cooled machine guns as its only armament and would be little use against conventional tanks in battle. The fact that the Nationalists were having to build their own armoured vehicles shows that they were not receiving the conventional heavy weaponry they needed. (Philip Jowett)

Opposite above: A Nationalist medium artillery unit moves through the streets of Shanghai on 17 May 1949. Their field gun is a slightly modified 75mm which appears to be an ex-Japanese model brought into Nationalist service in 1945. The outriders on the draught horses are armed with Mauser rifles, as was much of the Nationalist Army in the Civil War. (Philip Jowett)

Opposite below: The same artillery unit has a heavier gun in tow as the Nationalists build up their forces for the defence of Shanghai in May 1949. They are pulling a war booty 150mm Model 4 howitzer which is a Japanese gun added to the Nationalist armoury in 1945. Although the Nationalists received a lot of US equipment during the Civil War, they like the Communists used a large amount of Japanese artillery and tanks. (Philip Jowett)

Above: Nationalist troops rest in the streets of Shanghai as the People's Liberation Army moves into the city outskirts on 4 May. The soldier lying on his comrades' backpacks has his Thompson sub-machine gun propped between his legs. He and his friends are waiting for permission to take over the British-owned Cathay Hotel where they will be able to enjoy its luxuries. (Philip Jowett)

Opposite above: A Nationalist heavy howitzer fires towards People's Liberation Army lines in fighting for Shanghai in May 1949. The gun is an ex-Japanese Type 4 150mm howitzer which was gratefully received by the Nationalists in August 1945. There was a shortage of heavy artillery in both Nationalist and Communist armies so better Japanese guns like this were used until the end of the war. Some of the gun's crew are even wearing ex-Japanese cork sun helmets, which again would have been handed over to their troops in 1945. (Philip Jowett)

Opposite below: In May 1949 a unit of the Nationalist 'Disciplinary Corps' march through the outskirts of Shanghai. The Red Army were threatening the city and special units like this were employed to keep any Communist sympathisers in check. During the Civil War the Nationalists had to fight the enemy within as well as the Communist Army in the field. (Philip Jowett)

Above: Plain clothes Nationalist policemen execute their prisoners with a single bullet to the back of their heads in the streets of Shanghai. Their victims could be political enemies including Communists agitators, real or imagined, who were seen as a threat to Nationalist rule in the city. As the fall of the city approached there were executions like this on a daily basis usually on the streets in front of crowds. Anyone who spoke against the Nationalists or who suggested a Communist victory was punished, usually with a bullet. (Philip Jowett)

Opposite above: A Nationalist policemen executes his prisoner in public with a bullet from his revolver as a lesson to any bystanders who might be considering rebellion. Usually prisoners were carried through the streets with placards fastened to their backs describing their crimes. The expected fall of not only Shanghai but the rest of Nationalist China led to an increase in clamp downs on any kind of insurrection. (Philip Jowett)

Opposite below: This Nationalist policeman kills his prisoner with a single bullet from his Thompson sub-machine gun in Shanghai. Because Shanghai was the commercial centre of Nationalist China there was a large presence of armed police in the streets of the city. The paranoia in Shanghai against perceived threats from 'traitors' inside the city led to a sharp increase in executions. (Philip Jowett)

Communist troops clamber over a captured
Nationalist Type 97 medium tank in Shanghai which
had in turn had been captured from the Japanese
in August 1945. Although this model of tank was
outdated in 1945, it was gratefully received by
the Nationalists who put a number into service.
Both the Nationalists and Communists employed
Japanese personnel to crew these tanks during the
Civil War. (Philip Jowett)

Victorious Communist troops march into Shanghai
having seen the surrender of the city on 25 May 1949.
These confident troops have their rifles slung over
their shoulders, apart from the man in the foreground
who has a waxed umbrella over his. The umbrella was
a vital part of a Chinese soldier's kit for many years,
especially when there were so few tents to provide
shelter. Many of the troops also have canvas tubes of
rice as part of their equipment, carrying several days
of rations with them. (Philip Jowett)

Two People's Liberation Army Type 94 tankettes drive into Shanghai with their crews riding on them. The leading light tank has been adapted with the addition of a 20mm cannon on the front to add to the standard machine gun in the turret. Several of the crew have Imperial Army steel helmets to emphasise the importance of Japanese equipment to the Communist war effort. (Philip Jowett)

Above: A column of the 3rd Field Army under the command of General Chen Yi marches into Shanghai past the famous Park Hotel. As these victorious People's Liberation Army troops were marching into Shanghai 50,000 of the Nationalist garrison were withdrawing from the city by sea. The remaining 153,000 Nationalist troops were either killed or captured leaving behind them a large amount of war booty for the Communists. This was made up of 1,370 artillery pieces, including mortars, and 119 armoured vehicles, including tanks. The 1,161 trucks and other motor vehicles would give the People's Liberation Army much more mobility in the last few months of their campaign to defeat the Nationalists. (Philip Jowett)

Opposite: A tough-looking veteran of the Civil War is photographed in the streets of Shanghai in the last days of May 1949. Older soldiers like this man may have been fighting since at least 1937, first against the Japanese and then the Nationalists. Many of the rank and file of the People's Liberation Army were former Nationalist troops anyway, especially in the last year of the war. At times whole units of government troops went over to the Communists with their commanders, who accepted posts in the People's Liberation Army. (Philip Jowett)

People's Liberation Army soldiers move through the streets of newly 'liberated' Shanghai in search of Nationalist stragglers. The troops are a machine-gun team armed with old ZB-26 light machine guns and have their shovels at the ready to dig their weapon in. One man, with the raised shovel, looks rather warily at the camera while the rest of his team appears more relaxed. (Philip Jowett)

Chapter Eleven

The Long Retreat – Nationalist Defeats, 1949

The victorious People's Liberation Army spent a few months after their victory in the Huai-hai Campaign consolidating their hold on China, north of the Yangtze River. At the same time the Nationalists should have been spending time strengthening their defences on the southern bank of the river. The Nationalist command was distracted by the political struggles within its ranks, which included the resignation of Chiang Kai-shek in January 1949. For the rest of the war, Chiang and his replacement as President General Li Tsung-jen fell out among themselves. Chiang was now concentrating on sending as much money and resources to the island of Formosa where he had decided to establish a safe haven. He only saw the continued resistance of the Nationalist Army as a way of delaying the Communist victory until this withdrawal to Formosa had been completed.

The People's Liberation Army duly crossed the Yangtze on 20 April meeting with little resistance from the Nationalist defenders. Within a few days the Nationalist capital at Nanking had fallen and in the next month the major cities of Wuhan and Nanchang fell. Although the end of the war was near, there were still large Nationalist armies that had to be defeated by the People's Liberation Army. The Nationalists had hundreds of thousands of troops still in the field and some thought that these could be used to form a southern bastion. The idea was that in southern provinces like Kwangtung, Szechwan and Kwangsi a Nationalist stronghold could be established. In reality there was little chance of the People's Liberation Army's progress being halted apart from in isolated instances when the Nationalist Army made stands.

In mid-September Chiang Kai-shek made the drastic decision to order the withdrawal of all the remaining Nationalist forces north of Kwangtung province towards the city of Canton. He and his leadership had no faith in the poorly armed troops of Kwangtung to defend their province. The plan was simply to get as many of the better troops to southern ports so that they could be moved to the Nationalist bastion in Formosa. Chiang was desperately looking around for methods to 'stop the rot' and these included a plan to recruit 500 Japanese mercenaries, mainly made up of veteran pilots of the Imperial Air Force. By October 1949 there were approximately

200,000 Nationalist troops still in formations in the Southern provinces of China. Although these could have put up a reasonable fight if they had been motivated, in reality morale was low throughout the Nationalist Army.

Above: Wounded Nationalist soldiers arrive in Nanking on 15 April 1949 having taken part in a battle 35 miles to the east of the city. The last of the Nationalist garrison was to withdraw a week later and the city was left to the mobs, who looted large parts of it. Much to Chiang Kai-shek's dismay, his capital which had been his stronghold since the late 1920s fell without much of a fight. The People's Liberation Army did not reach the city without losses, with an estimated 10,000 being killed in air raids by the Nationalist Air Force as they advanced. When the Communists moved into the city on the 23rd the Nationalist capital had already been moved to Canton in Kwangtung province. (Philip Jowett)

Opposite above: Chiang Kai-shek leaves the National Assembly in Nanking in January 1949 after making a speech to his troops, who now acclaim him. Over the next few months the Nationalists began to withdraw southwards towards their political heartland in the southern provinces. Chiang still had the support of many in his army and a minority of the Chinese population. As the defeats mounted during the year this support slipped away and many just wanted the war to end regardless of who was victorious. (Philip Jowett)

Opposite below: In early February 1949 the Nationalist Navy patrols the Yangtze River at Nanking with the Communist Army concentrating on its north bank. These ships are keeping the crossings of the river open so that any Nationalist troops on the opposite bank could escape. The two ships are the *Chang Chi* on the left of the photograph and the *Chu Yu* on the right-hand side. Of the twelve Nationalist Navy's ships assigned to defend Nanking, only four escaped to fight another day. The other eight were taken over by the newly organised People's Liberation Navy along with their crews to man them for their new 'masters'. (Philip Jowett)

Above: General Wang Yu-chi, the Nationalist commander of the garrison of the city of Chinkiang in Kiangsu province, joins a sentry at his strongpoint in April 1949. Most Nationalist garrison commanders in 1949 claimed that they would defend their city or town 'to the last man'. In reality most generals either surrendered after a token fight against the People's Liberation Army or negotiated with the enemy before they attacked. This posed propaganda picture belies the poor relationship between the Nationalist soldier and his officer. There were only a few exceptional Nationalist officers who had a good rapport with their men and General Wang may have been one of them. (Philip Jowett)

Opposite above: Smiling Nationalist officers are moving around the streets of Nanking riding on the bare frame of a US-supplied jeep. As the People's Liberation Army drew closer to the former Nationalist capital the main priority of officers like this would be to get out of the city. It was only the 'diehards' in the Nationalist Army who believed that the war was winnable or even sustainable. These officers have had to improvise their transport as much of the US-supplied aid had been lost to the Communists. (Philip Jowett)

Opposite below: People's Liberation Army troops march into Nanking on 23 April after the relative peaceful handover of power by the Nationalists. Just like during the Sino-Japanese War, the 40ft high wall that ran for 20 miles around the city was no protection for the city. When the People's Liberation Army arrived at the city's gates they were left open by the Nationalist garrison and the Communists marched in. An assault was staged for the propaganda cameras to satisfy the Communist need for a suitably revolutionary victory. (Philip Jowett)

Above: This force of well-equipped and well-armed Nationalist Marines are being transported by a US-supplied landing craft to try and keep a river open to government traffic in 1949. Formed in 1914, the Chinese Marines were by 1945 a sizeable force which was trained and equipped by the USA. Some of the Marines are armed with the M3 'grease gun' sub-machine guns which were supplied in large numbers to the Nationalists after 1945. They have also been issued with M2 steel helmets which were usually only worn by the better Nationalist units. (Philip Jowett)

Opposite above: A Nationalist sentry guards the population of the fortified city of Chinkiang who have been recruited to help dig entrenchments and firing points for its garrison in mid-1949. As the Communist advance continued many Nationalist held towns and cities in their way were fortified in this manner. With their defensive attitude the Nationalists should have been well used to building fortifications. In reality these positions more often than not were not defended by the garrison when the People's Liberation Army arrived at their gates. (Philip Jowett)

Opposite below: This parade of the artillery of the Muslim Nationalist warlord of the Western Chinese province of Ninghsia in early May 1949 looks impressive at first sight. In reality some of the artillery limbers do not have guns attached and the field guns in the photograph are an older model. The commander, General Ma Hung-'kuei, relied heavily on his cavalry who had a reputation for reckless bravery and their hatred of all Communists. Ma's troops would be swept away by the People's Liberation Army when they finally arrived in Ninghsia, one of the remotest provinces in China. (US National Archives)

A young naval infantryman of the forces fighting along the rivers of China stands guard over his barracks in 1949. As in earlier wars in China, the river network was important to the outcome of the war as men and equipment were moved along them. Both sides used motorised junks to transport their troops, while the Nationalists had a number of former Japanese river gunboats. (Philip Jowett)

Nationalist troops of the 4th Army withdraw from Canton in Kwangtung province in October 1949. By this stage in the Civil War the Nationalist retreat had reached the pro-Nationalist southern provinces of China. These troops of the 80,000-strong garrison are some of the last Nationalist soldiers still left on the mainland who had kept their discipline. Attempts at forming a southern Nationalist bastion came to nothing. The usual rivalries and divisions within the army meant that in most cases it was now 'every man for himself'. (Philip Jowett)

A Communist cavalryman is photographed in an official image wearing the summer version of the People's Liberation Army uniform. During the 1937–45 Sino-Japanese War the Communists made great use of their mounted units. They organised these into columns that often operated far behind Japanese lines. The veterans of the pre-1945 units were now joined by young volunteers from among the Northern Chinese population. In 1949 they had to face the wild Muslim horsemen of the Nationalist warlords of Western China. During a number of battles in North-Western China in the closing phases they were to meet their match. Although the Nationalist cavalry recorded a number of significant victories over the Communists, these were not enough to stop the advance of the People's Liberation Army into Kansu and Ninghsia provinces. (Philip Jowett)

Above: Muslim militiamen from the western province of Ninghsia who are still loyal to the Nationalist governor of the province, General Ma Hung-kui, parade in 1949. The irregulars are wearing white uniforms with special insignia above the breast pockets of their shirts and their own Muslim skull caps. These Muslim troops were fanatically anti-Communist and continued to fight until the end for Chiang Kai-shek. (Philip Jowett)

Opposite above: HMS *Amethyst*, a British Royal Navy ship, was sailing from Shanghai to Nanking to take over the role of guard ship for the British Embassy. While travelling along the Yangtze River in April 1949 it came under Communist artillery fire and was forced to run aground. As a consequence, twenty-two of the crew were killed and eleven wounded by the shelling and the *Amethyst* was left under threat by the People's Liberation Army for several months. It was finally evacuated in late July after several rescue attempts by other British ships. This so-called Amethyst Incident was a foretaste of the hostility of the Chinese Communists to the Western Powers after their victory in 1949. (Philip Jowett)

Opposite below: Nationalist Muslim militiamen in the remote western province of Ninghsia are given basic military instruction. All the Nationalist military governors in North-Western China were Muslim and they had a real hatred of Communism. The control of some of the remoter provinces of China by the Nationalists continued until the very end of the war. This was only because the People's Liberation Army could not physically advance fast enough across the vast distances of China. (Philip Jowett)

Soldiers of the Muslim warlord General Ma Pu-fang are seen in the border area of Tibet and Western China. It was only in the remotest regions of Western China that the People's Liberation Army was being resisted by the end of 1949. In this region the military leadership were all Muslims and fiercely anti-Communist, including Ma Pu-fang. Ma was more than happy personally to execute whole regiments of Communist captives either by pistol or by sword. Although the Muslim cavalry won some of the last Nationalist victories of the Civil War in 1949, these successes would not turn the tide. (Philip Jowett)

General Li Tsung-jen, the recently installed President of Nationalist China, is featured in a patriotic poster. Chiang Kai-shek resigned the presidency on 4 January 1949 and Li was handed the 'poisoned chalice' of the leadership of the already doomed Nationalist China. He took a few days to accept the post as he wasn't sure he had the backing of the other Nationalist leaders. He was seen as a more acceptable person to negotiate with the Communists but Mao was too near to victory to talk to Li. (Philip Jowett)

Chairman Mao Tse-tung announces the formation of the Chinese People's Republic on 1 October 1949 from a rostrum in Tiananmen Square in Peking. His speech included the phrase that 'China has stood up' and called for the support of the Chinese people behind his movement. The Communist victory did not end the suffering of the Chinese people and for many it meant death or imprisonment. Others welcomed the Communist victory which freed them from corrupt and incompetent government. Mao brought in policies that tried quickly to change aspects of life that had been part of traditional Chinese life for centuries. It is estimated that millions also died as a result of Mao's austere policies which caused famines in some regions of the country. (Philip Jowett)

At a bustling Southern Chinese port Nationalist troops are being embarked onto their navy's ships for evacuation to Formosa. Chiang Kai-shek removed some of his best remaining military assets to the island which was to be the Nationalists' home base from early 1950. On the harbour-side are a row of T-26 light tanks, survivors of the eighty or so bought from the Soviet Union in 1937–8. Once the Nationalists established themselves on Formosa more modern US tanks would soon replace these obsolete ones. (Philip Jowett)

Chapter Twelve

Communist Victory –
The Fall of the South, 1949

The Communist advance became a procession with Nationalist held cities and towns falling like a row of dominoes. By September 1949 the Nationalist government in Canton was under threat largely from sizeable Communist guerrilla forces in the region. During early October the regular Communist People's Liberation Army advanced on Canton capturing the last mountain range before the city. This caused a great deal of panic in the city with government officials packing their bags. Government offices were evacuated to the next projected temporary capital at remote Chungking, the 1938–45 wartime capital of the Nationalists. Even though the resistance of the Nationalist Army was crumbling some units did put up a fight as the People's Liberation Army moved through Southern China. For instance the Nationalists lost 58,000 during their fighting against the People's Liberation Army's advance through Kwangtung province. These losses were in vain as the Communists took forty cities and towns during their campaign. Canton fell on 15 October with the nearby port of Amoy falling on the 17th. The garrison of Amoy retreated to the island of Quemoy where ten days later they were able to defeat a People's Liberation Army landing there. This was one of a handful of victories that the Nationalists won during the fighting in the South, in fact some sources describe this as the only victory of 1949.

The Nationalist government had left Canton for the wartime capital at Chungking on the 12th. A month later General Li Tsung-jen left for Hong Kong having lost faith in Chiang and the Nationalists. In the final days of the war Chiang landed by plane at Chungking and took control once more of the remnants of the government. On 29 November Chiang and his entourage left Chungking for the final temporary capital at Chengtu. From there Chiang flew to Taipei on Formosa and established the new capital of the Nationalist government on 9 December. The People's Liberation Army had now completed its victory and had proved its mettle in its long struggle with the Nationalists. Despite many setbacks the People's Liberation Army had out-fought and out-thought Chiang's army and overcome overwhelming odds to achieve their victory. Fighting countless battles and marching for thousands of miles, the People's Liberation Army was now the master of China. Between November 1948 and November 1949 the People's Liberation Army advanced 2,000 miles from Mukden in Manchuria to Canton in Kwangtung province.

A column of Nationalist prisoners including some women soldiers or nurses move towards a prison camp. There they will be processed by the People's Liberation Army's intelligence and propaganda personnel to assess their loyalty to Chiang Kai-shek. Ordinary soldiers were seldom punished for fighting for the Nationalists, although officers were often poorly treated. Their best hope would be to be sent to re-education camps where after going through various courses most would eventually be released. (Philip Jowett)

More Nationalist troops move southwards in the autumn of 1949 in the hope that they can join the evacuation of their forces from the mainland to Formosa. If they do not manage to reach their own lines, their alternative is to surrender to the Communists. This group of soldiers includes a few females who may be nurses or 'camp followers' who have adopted uniforms to get on the army's ration list. It looks like these troops have abandoned their weapons and have given up all hope of resisting the victorious People's Liberation Army. The politically reliable Nationalist troops had already been evacuated to Formosa with 100,000 of them in the south of the island by mid-1949. (Philip Jowett)

Soldiers of the People's Liberation Army take a well-earned meal break during their advance through the remaining Nationalist held territory. These troops are wearing the basic uniform still in use with a large number of the Communist forces. On the front of their caps is the simple red star which was the universal symbol of the Red Army regardless of rank. (Philip Jowett)

Above: Soldiers of the People's Liberation Army celebrate yet another victory in their advance through Southern China in the second half of 1949. The People's Liberation Army had been moulded into a tough fighting machine over four years of war and had proved superior to its Nationalist foes. In the aftermath of the Civil War many of these troops would be surplus to requirements with large numbers of ex-Nationalist troops being disbanded as potentially unreliable. (Philip Jowett)

Opposite above: This landlord shares the fate of thousands of landowners at the hands of the Communists in the aftermath of their victory. On many occasions the deaths of landlords were popular with the local peasants who had suffered at their hands. Other landlords who hadn't persecuted their tenants were also killed by the Communists who wanted to eradicate this class from the 'new' China. (Philip Jowett)

Opposite below: In the aftermath of an execution of 'hated' landlords in the Chinese countryside the Communist executioners stand over their victims. Figures for the number of class enemies killed in the days and months after the Civil War are unreliable. Local Communist leaders organised the killing of Nationalist officials and civilians who were seen as true 'enemies of the people'. Others were given re-education to convince them of the error of their ways in their former support for Chiang Kai-shek and his government. (Philip Jowett)

Above: This US-produced bubblegum card shows the American view of the 'red peril' facing China in the Civil War. According to this card, People's Liberation Army machine-gunners routinely killed Red Cross workers who were evacuating wounded Nationalist soldiers from the battlefield. This kind of propaganda was in its own way as biased as that issued by the Communists during the 1940s and 1950s. Atrocities were committed by both sides during the Civil War and by the Communists afterwards. (Philip Jowett)

Opposite: A propaganda postcard from the end of the Civil War shows a flag bearer and rifleman of the People's Liberation Army. Both men wear the light khaki cotton uniform which was worn by some soldiers in both armies. Their headgear is based on the pre-1945 field cap worn by the Nationalist Army and they wear red armbands to distinguish them from their enemies. The rifle is a Johnson M1941 which was produced at the same time as the US Garand M1 rifle but did not see widespread service. It appears to have been supplied in large numbers to the Nationalist Army during the Civil War and this man's has come from that source. (Philip Jowett)

This mixed group of Nationalist prisoners and People's Liberation Army captors shows the shift in power and in the resources available to each combatant by the end of the war. The soldiers in the steel helmets supplied by the USA are in fact Communist troops while those in the field caps are Nationalists! By early 1949 many Nationalist formations were going over to the People's Liberation Army and some received payments for doing so. One 5,000-strong Nationalist unit was offered 2 silver dollars per man to join their nearest People's Liberation Army unit. When they found out that there were only enough dollars for 3,000 men the other 2,000 returned to their Nationalist unit the next morning! (Philip Jowett)

Chapter Thirteen

The Aftermath, 1950-4

As the remaining Nationalist armies retreated in front of the advancing People's Liberation Army most units had little choice but to surrender to the victorious Communists. During the final months of the fighting the Communists claimed that 157,000 Nationalists had given up without a fight. Others who were close to the Chinese borders decided to take refuge in various neighbouring territories. Some 100,000 crossed by boat to the island of Hainan where they found temporary shelter before the arrival of a People's Liberation Army invasion force. A group of 25,000 Nationalist troops crossed from Yunnan province into French Indo-China where some fought for the French against the Viet-Minh. Another 15,000 or so crossed into newly independent Burma where they set up their own enclaves keeping the Burmese Army out. In the 1950s they made a number of raids into China but lost interest when it became apparent that the Communists were here to stay. Some got involved in the local drugs trade and formed an army that fought against the Burmese into the 1960s. Any other Nationalist hold-outs that continued fighting after 1950 were soon isolated and mopped up. With little chance of receiving aid from the government on Taiwan any Nationalist political or military opposition to the People's Republic was doomed.

The withdrawal of the Nationalist government and the remnants of its army to Taiwan did not end the conflict in China. Although the Civil War was over and the Communists were victorious, the rivalry between Chiang and Mao was not at an end. In fact, it was to continue until the deaths of the two leaders in the mid-1970s, twenty-five years later. Chiang expected his stay on Taiwan to be temporary as he thought that conflict between the USA and the Soviet Union was inevitable. This conflict, Chiang thought, would involve Communist China on the side of the Russians allowing his Nationalist Army to re-enter the fray on the side of the USA.

The island of Taiwan was under the leadership of Chiang Kai-shek, who had taken up his former position as President of Nationalist China on 1 March 1950. His scheme to form an alliance with the USA did not go according to plan even when they were at war with Communist China in Korea from 1950. Chiang appealed to the USA, which was fighting as part of the United Nations forces, to let him send Nationalist troops to fight on the mainland. His request was politely turned down as this could have led to the intervention of the Soviet Union in the Korean War.

The People's Republic of China began to plan military campaigns to 'liberate' the offshore islands which were under Nationalist control. Those islands close to the Chinese coast were most vulnerable with the large island of Hainan taken by a 100,000-strong invasion force in April 1950. Other islands, such as the Choushan Islands a few miles off the Chekiang coast, had to be evacuated in May 1950. Other islands were successfully defended by Nationalist garrisons which were under regular bombardment from the mainland. At the same time commando operations were launched from Nationalist held islands into China in the 1950s.

In October 1950 the People's Liberation Army invaded Tibet against a backdrop of worldwide condemnation as Mao decided to reclaim all territories that had formed part of the pre-1911 Empire. Mao's ambitions were backed by a military force that in sheer size was a threat to any nation in Eastern Asia. The victorious People's Liberation Army had grown from only 90,000 in 1937 to a force of many millions of men. In 1950 the People's Liberation Army had an official strength of 5,000,000 men and women with an estimated 'hardcore' of 1,000,000 men. Its elite was made up of the 18th Group Army with 600,000 men, many who were veterans of the 1930s. A total of 75 per cent of the People's Liberation Army's weapons and equipment were of US origin, while other weapons were worn out ex-Japanese items. There were 200 full-strength divisions with another 125 divisions that were below full strength and varied greatly in size from 2,000 to 25,000 men. There was another fifty divisions in training and being equipped with the vast stocks of captured weapons and equipment. The People's Liberation Air Force was being supplied with 800 Soviet aircraft, including some 'brand-new' MIG-15 jet fighter bombers. There were also 200 fighter bombers and 100 medium bombers of older Soviet types along with hundreds of ex-US planes.

Although during the 1950s the Nationalist Army on Taiwan had built up its strength gradually, it was able to hold off an invasion of the island. During the 1960s and early 1970s the amount of modern weaponry received by the Taiwan government increased. By the mid-1970s the Nationalist Army on Taiwan had reached the strength of 420,000 men with 800 modern tanks. This force was strong enough to discourage an invasion by the People's Liberation Army but not nearly strong enough to threaten the Chinese People's Republic.

A smart Nationalist sentry stands guard over an airfield with two T-6 Texan trainers on the island of Hainan in early 1950. Hainan, just off the Southern Chinese coastline, proved impossible to defend against the People's Liberation Army when it attacked in April 1950. The well-established Communist guerrilla movement on the island made it difficult for the 120,000-strong garrison to defend it. A 12,000-strong People's Liberation Army assault force landed in mid-April and was soon able to defeat the demoralised Nationalist troops. (Philip Jowett)

Newly evacuated Nationalist troops undergo training at a camp on the island of Formosa in 1950. They have been issued with new uniforms but are still armed with Mauser 98k rifles which may have been in service since the 1930s. The forces which were taken off the mainland spent much of the early 1950s fighting off Communist attempts to conquer islands controlled by the Nationalists. (Philip Jowett)

Above: People's Liberation Army troops wade ashore from their junk on the Choushan Islands in May 1950. The fall of a number of offshore islands held by the Nationalists in the aftermath of the Communist victory was unstoppable. Some islands were heavily defended by the Nationalists, while others had to be conceded as they realised that it was pointless to fight for them. Shortages of weaponry on the Communist side are evident in the use by these troops of British Sten guns captured by the People's Liberation Army during the Civil War. (Philip Jowett)

Opposite above: People's Liberation Army troops come ashore from their invasion junks on the island of Hainan in April 1950. The invasion of the large island just off the Southern Chinese coast was another success for the Communists. Although the Nationalists had a strong garrison on the island with 120,000 men, 45 aircraft and 50 ships, they could not hold it. By 24 April the island had fallen with the Nationalists suffering heavy casualties of 33,000 men while 90,000 were evacuated by sea. In contrast, the official losses of the People's Liberation Army assault force of about 120,000 were only 4,500 men, although these were almost certainly much higher. (Philip Jowett)

Opposite below: People's Liberation Army troops march through the Tibetan mountains to take control of the remote region claimed by the new Chinese People's Republic in early October 1950. The 40,000-strong force was described by the Communists as a liberating army and by the vast majority of Tibetans as invaders. Carrying portraits of Mao Tse-tung, the People's Liberation Army expected little opposition to their 'Peaceful Lberation'. To their surprise the Chinese met a great deal of resistance to their take-over of Tibet and had a hard fight against 4,000 Tibetan troops in the Chamdo region. Low-level guerrilla resistance continued well into the 1960s with covert support from the Central Intelligence Agency. (Philip Jowett)

These Tibetan soldiers are typical of the troops that faced the People's Liberation Army in October 1950. The 10,000-strong Tibetan Army had been trained by British instructors in the 1930s and was armed with Lee–Enfield rifles and Bren and Lewis light machine guns. They also had a few mountain guns sold to them by the British Indian Authorities before the Second World War. This poorly armed and trained army was no match regardless of individual bravery for the hardened veterans of the People's Liberation Army. (Philip Jowett)

Young cadets of the Nationalist Army demonstrate in support of Chiang Kai-shek from their new base on the island of Taiwan, 1950. Nearly all the Chinese refugees who went to Taiwan were fully behind Chiang and many were the families of Nationalist leaders and military commanders. The indigenous population of the island were against all foreign invaders and had to be subdued by the Nationalist Army. In 1947 they rebelled against the presence of Chinese 'aliens' on their island and were ruthlessly suppressed by Chiang's troops. (Philip Jowett)

我们一定要解放台湾

A Communist propaganda poster from the early 1950s shows the Chinese people and army symbolically invading the last refuge of Chiang Kai-shek and his clique on Formosa. By this time Formosa was commonly known as Taiwan, which had been the name used in China for a number of years. The towering heroic Communist figures bearing down on the island are in contrast to the cowering Chiang and his equally puny US ally. Unlike the Nationalist held islands just off the coast of mainland China, Formosa was a more difficult 'nut' for the Communists to 'crack'. There is no doubt that the Communists would have invaded Formosa, or Taiwan as it was renamed, if it had been possible in the early years of the revolution. (Philip Jowett)

Above: Two People's Liberation Army soldiers look across the Yalu River into neighbouring North Korea. The division of Korea into a Communist North and a pro-Western South created a front line in Asia in the new Cold War. When the North Koreans invaded the South in 1950 their initial success turned into a rout and their retreat northwards. As the United Nations military forces led by the US moved into North Korea Mao Tse-tung decided to intervene decisively. The Chinese People's Republic was on its knees and Mao's energies would have been better directed into trying to build his new nation. His solution was to send many thousands of 'volunteers' into North Korea to fight alongside his Communist allies there. (Gavin Goh)

Opposite above: Although this photograph is often attributed to the Civil War period, it is more likely from the Chinese intervention in Korea from 1950 until 1953. Hundreds of thousands of People's Volunteers were sent by the Communist leadership to attack South Korean and US forces during the war. Mao Tse-tung hoped that his support for the North Koreans would result in a powerful ally on his border. The 'Chinese People's Volunteer Army' was a proxy force which no one was under any illusions was organised and armed by the Chinese government. These 'volunteers' are armed with captured US 105mm howitzers and, in the background, ex-Japanese guns. (Philip Jowett)

Opposite below: Some of the first Communist Chinese prisoners taken in the Korean War are brought out of their prison to face the press. The thousands of Chinese 'volunteers' who fought in the Korean War were often veterans of the Civil War but others were raw recruits. These men are wearing the new quilted winter uniform which many had on when they crossed the Yalu River in October 1950. Some Chinese volunteers refused to surrender as their officers had told them that the United Nations troops would execute any prisoners. This was part of the propaganda issued by the People's Republic to convince their soldiers that the USA and the West were the main enemies. (Philip Jowett)

Above: In the first few years of the Nationalist regime being set up on the island of Taiwan some military resources were in short supply. These Nationalist recruits are wearing improvised uniforms made up of old-fashioned cotton shirt and trousers. They are wearing them with locally produced hats in lieu of field caps or steel helmets and are armed with Mauser rifles brought over from mainland China. (Philip Jowett)

Opposite above: In the early 1950s this parade of truck-mounted troops shows the continued reliance of the People's Liberation Army on war-booty weapons and equipment. The machine guns are mostly ex-Canadian Bren guns, while the helmets are former Japanese M32s. Although the rows of trucks full of well-armed troops may look impressive, mass attacks launched by the Chinese in Korea showed that the People's Liberation Army needed to modernise as a priority. (Philip Jowett)

Opposite below: This line-up of ex-Japanese Type 97 tanks are on parade in one of the shows of strength which the People's Republic of China revelled in. The fact that all these tanks are of 1930s' vintage shows some of the weaknesses that the People's Liberation Army had. In the early to mid-1950s the Soviet Union began to supply modern tanks, artillery and especially jet aircraft to bolster their forces. (Philip Jowett)

Above: This Nationalist soldier in Burma in the early 1950s is part of a renegade army that crossed the Burmese–Chinese border at the end of the Civil War in 1950. The so-called 'Yunnan Anti-Communist National Salvation Army' was commanded by General Li Mi. From an initial force of 1,500 troops it grew to a maximum strength of 6,000 supported by the CIA, Thailand and the Nationalist government in Taiwan. After a period of raids into Communist Chinese territory the Nationalist force began to get involved in the Burmese opium trade. The unhappy Burmese government launched military campaigns against the Nationalist Army jointly with the People's Liberation Army in the early 1960s. A few groups survived in Burma until the 1980s but by that time had lost their association with Nationalist China. (Philip Jowett)

Opposite: This propaganda photograph from the early 1950s shows a People's Liberation Army tank driver wearing a mixture of Japanese and Chinese uniform. His fur-lined crash helmet is either Japanese or a copy of a captured one and made by a Chinese workshop. The overalls he wears are probably made in a government factory as captured stores began to be exhausted. He is driving a Soviet T-26 light tank which has had a colourful history to say the least. It was first supplied to Nationalist China in the late 1930s as part of about eighty sold by the Soviet Union. They went onto serve in Burma in 1941 and a few survived to serve in the Civil War in both Nationalist and Communist hands. For a short period after Mao's victory these now hopefully out of date and well-worn tanks would have still been used by the People's Liberation Army. (Philip Jowett)

Above: A M4 Sherman tank of the Nationalist Army rumbles through the streets of Taipei in the early 1950s. US support for Chiang Kai-shek on his island stronghold increased in the early 1950s as the Cold War progressed. The entry of Mao's Communist China in the Korean War meant that Chiang was now seen as an ally in the new world order. Tanks like the M4 had never been supplied to the Nationalists during the Civil War but were now sent to them in large numbers. (Gavin Goh)

Opposite above: These Yunnanese Communist Women Militia are on parade in the early 1950s wearing their traditional provincial dress. The new Communist government was determined to prove that it had the support of all the regions and provinces of China. This kind of propaganda was intended to reinforce the image that China was now united behind Chairman Mao. Although most of the women here are armed with ex-Nationalist Mausers, the woman on the left appears to have a Japanese Arisaka rifle. (Philip Jowett)

Opposite below: The massed ranks of the Chinese Nationalist Army parade in Taipei, the capital of Taiwan, in the mid-1950s. By this time the Nationalist soldier was well equipped, armed and trained and prepared to defend the island from Communist invasion. The air force had received modern jet fighters and bombers and the army had tanks and artillery from the USA. (Philip Jowett)

At the end of the Civil War huge amounts of weaponry and equipment fell into Communist hands. In the first few years after victory the People's Liberation Army, Navy and Air Force used some of this 'war booty'. These former Nationalist Mustang P-51 fighters would only be kept in service until the MIG-15 jet fighters were acquired from the Soviet Union in sufficient numbers. (Philip Jowett)

This Communist poster 'pulls no punches' as it proclaims the coming take-over of Taiwan by the People's Liberation Army, Navy and Air Force. As the air and naval forces move towards the island Chiang Kai-shek and his symbolic US supporter cower in fear of the 'glorious' invasion. Any invasion of the Nationalist bastion would have been extremely bloody and costly for both sides. In reality the protection of the US Fleet made any Communist attack impractical in the 1950s. While other Nationalist held islands close to the mainland could be taken by invasion armadas made up mainly of junks, Taiwan was too far from the Chinese mainland and too well protected to be easily taken by such improvised fleets. (Philip Jowett)

A soldier of the Chinese Nationalist Army on Taiwan takes part in one of the continuous and rigorous training exercises on the island in the 1950s. The Taiwanese population, which was largely made up of refugees from mainland China, was accustomed to a siege mentality. During the 1950s and 1960s Chiang Kai-shek and his people were in constant fear of an all-out invasion of their anti-Communist enclave. This soldier shows the mix of older weaponry and modern equipment seen in service with the Nationalist Army in the 1950s. (Philip Jowett)

The bugler of a Nationalist unit takes part in one of the incessant training sessions on the island of Taiwan in the early 1950s. After the Communist Chinese intervention in the Korean War of 1950–3 the Nationalist government on Taiwan could expect more material aid. New tanks like the M41 bulldog and jet fighters like the F86 Sabre would arrive in the 1950s and 1960s. The Nationalist Army, Navy and Air Force were built up by the USA as an ally in the Cold War in the Far East. (Philip Jowett)

In 1958 Nationalist troops sit in a trench on the disputed island of Kinmen during the 2nd Taiwan Strait Crisis. The island, which was off the coast of Fukien province, had been invaded in 1949 by an improvised Communist armada. It was the successful defence of Kinmen which secured Taiwan from invasion at least temporarily. There was constant pressure on the island throughout the 1950s which was relieved through diplomacy at the end of the 1958 crisis. These troops have been well supplied with US small arms, including M2 carbines and a bazooka. (Philip Jowett)